ABDULLAH AHMAD BADAWI
Revivalist of an Intellectual Tradition

Published by
Pelanduk Publications (M) Sdn Bhd
(Co. No. 113307-W)
12 Jalan SS13/3E
Subang Jaya Industrial Estate
47500 Subang Jaya
Selangor Darul Ehsan, Malaysia

Address all correspondence to
Pelanduk Publications (M) Sdn Bhd
P.O. Box 8265, 46785 Kelana Jaya
Selangor Darul Ehsan, Malaysia

Website: *www.pelanduk.com*
e-mail: *rusaone@tm.net.my*

Perpustakaan Negara Malaysia   Cataloguing-in-Publication Data

Al-Attas, Syed Ali Tawfik
    Abdullah Ahmad Badawi: revivalist of an intellectual tradition / Syed
    Ali Tawfik al-Attas, Ng Tieh Chuan.
    Includes index
    Bibliography: p. 149
    ISBN 967-978-911-X
    1. Abdullah Haji Ahmad Badawi, Dato' Seri, 1939- — Contributions
    in Islam. 2. Islam and state—Malaysia. 3. Malaysia—Politics and
    government. I. Ng. Tieh Chuan. II. Title.
    297.272092

Printed and bound in Malaysia

ABDULLAH
AHMAD BADAWI
Revivalist of an Intellectual Tradition

SYED ALI TAWFIK AL-ATTAS
NG TIEH CHUAN

Pelanduk
Publications

Dato' Seri Abdullah bin Haji Ahmad Badawi

Datin Paduka Seri Endon binti Mahmood

Dato' Haji Ahmad bin Haji Abdullah
(popularly referred to as Ahmad Badawi)

Haji Abdullah bin Haji Ibrahim
(popularly referred to as Abdullah Fahim)

Dato' Seri Abdullah with his late mother,
Dato' Kailan Hassan

DATO' MOHAMED ABID

FOREWORD

Since the establishment of Malaysia as an independent sovereign nation, it has become clear that the most urgent problem of multicultural and multiracial Malaysia, is the integration and assimilation of its various peoples and cultures into a modern developed nation. The cultural influences of the Middle East, China, India, and most recently the modern Western world have invariably left their indelible seals on Malaysia as the most significant melting-pot of the more consequential cultural traditions in history. It is, therefore, vital for the aforementioned diverse cultural groups to understand their individual roles if a harmonious compromise is to prevail.

Formulated upon this premise, therefore, the authors conclude that the problem for the Muslims as we understand it today, is one of identity. It is only by virtue of correct definition that one may arrive at true meaning, which is the cornerstone of knowledge. Hence, I am pleased to commend this book. The presentation of the structure and concept of the great worldview of Islam in comparison with those of other cultural traditions and their present day manifestations, along with their relevance in Malaysia, will lend not only an insight into the complex problems suffered by the Muslims, but may also provide the social and political engineer with the relevant material in his attempts to develop the growing Malaysian populace.

The author's concise detailed academic judgement in a language both lucid and illuminating concerning the phrase 'Islam hadhari', will undoubtedly render this work a reference manual, available to the modern Muslim world in general, one in which Malaysia is looked upon as being a representation of the tradition of learning and tolerance.

Dato' Mohamed Abid
Kuala Lumpur
31st January, 2005

Contents

Ku Cari Damai Abadi[*]

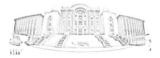

Aku cari bukan harta bertimbun-timbun
Untuk hidup kaya
Aku cari bukan wang berjuta-juta
Untuk hidup bergaya
Aku cari bukan kawan-kawan
Untuk hidup sekadar berfoya-foya
Aku cari mana dia al-Ghazzālī
Aku cari mana dia al-Shāfi ʿī
Kita bongkar rahsia kitab suci
Cari panduan
Kita bongkar rahsia sunnah nabi
Cari pedoman
Aku hidup kerana Dia, Rabbi
Dialah teman
Dialah wali
Dia mencukupi
Aku hidup bererti
Menikmati damai abadi.

---

[*] The following is the original version of Abdullah Ahmad Badawi's poem translated as "In Search of Everlasting Peace", written in the Malay language, which he recited on the 9th of May 2003.

In Search of Everlasting Peace

I seek not riches untold
To live a life of luxury
I seek not millions
To live a life of plenty
I seek not friends so many
To live a life of profligacy
I seek he who is al-Ghazzālī
I seek he who is al-Shāfiʿī
To unravel the secrets in the Holy Book
Seeking guidance
To unravel the secrets in the ways of the Prophet
Seeking direction
I live only for Him, my Lord
He is my Companion
He is my Witness
He suffices
I live a life full of meaning
Immersed in everlasting peace.

Abdullah Ahmad Badawi
9th May 2003

Acknowledgement

IT IS NORMAL practice to recognise those individuals deemed most helpful to the writers throughout the duration of their research, either in the preface, the prologue, or in a separate acknowledgement page. We have, wherever possible, fulfilled this task in both the prefatory introduction and the prologue. So, one may ask, why do we still feel it necessary to once again create a special page purely for gratuitous appreciation?

This project was conceived over a period spanning three stages. The original draft required the assistance of certain individuals who have been duly recognised for their contributions in the prefatory introduction. Since the original draft was subjected to further revision, it became incumbent to offer appreciation to those individuals most deserving of recognition, and hence the prologue. After the manuscript was complete, the authors sought the approval and blessing of the Prime Minister, who read the entire manuscript and offered his insights in order to further enhance the work. One in particular, was concerned with his poem, "In Search of Everlasting Peace", already in circulation. He had expressed concern over the fact that in two places, the sentences were reversed. As such, he suggested we make the necessary amendments.

Therefore, it is with great pleasure that we offer our profound gratitude to the Prime Minister, Dato' Seri Abdullah Haji Ahmad Badawi, for his help in reading and scrutinising the manuscript. In addition, we wish to thank the Prime Minister's brothers, Dato' Ibrahim Ahmad and Mr. Mohammad Tahir Ahmad for their kind assistance and for furnishing us with photographs of their father and grandfather. We are also grateful to the Principal Private Secretary to the Prime Minister, Dato' Mohamed Thajudeen Abdul Wahab, for all his efforts.

Finally, our esteemed appreciation is reserved for Dato' Mohamed Abid, who, at the behest of the Prime Minister, his personal friend, accepted the invitation to write the foreword to this book and for providing the photograph of the Prime Minister with his late mother.

Prefatory Introduction

THIS BOOK WAS originally entitled *Abdullah: A Profile in Integrity*, because at the time, it was an apt description of a leader who was never a political sycophant. As a politician with real integrity, Abdullah Haji Ahmad Badawi has always made his own decisions and accepted responsibility for them, even when this meant serving time in the political wilderness. In the process, he earned the respect of those who initially opposed him but later recognised his personal qualities and felt obliged to support his rise to the highest political office in the country.

Abdullah: A Profile in Integrity was written as an introduction to the political journey of Abdullah Haji Ahmad Badawi, the fifth Prime Minister of Malaysia. Abdullah has been in politics and government for a long time and has a reputation for being an honest and God-fearing person. He once said, "ultimately the accountability for my life rests with Allāh the Almighty".

As a publisher, I have wanted to publish a book tracing the political life of Abdullah since 1991, when he was appointed Minister of Foreign Affairs. Here was someone I admired and continue to admire. Over time I had come to know him and had developed a healthy respect for him. Moreover, there were hardly any books published on him, even though he was already a public figure. This was the same feeling I had way back in late 1981, while managing a foreign owned publishing firm in Malaysia. I had made a similar decision then, but the book was to be on Tun Dr. Mahathir Mohamad, the former Prime Minister who was the Deputy Prime Minister at the time. I managed to commission the late J. Victor Morais to write the book entitled *Mahathir: A Profile in Courage*, which was published in 1982, several months after he assumed the highest post in government as the fourth Prime Minister of Malaysia.

With regard to the originally proposed publication on Abdullah, I started commissioning writers in 1991. Unfortunately, there were few who showed interest in the project, and those that did express an interest, never went further than the contents page. Some cited a shortage of reference materials available in the various research institutions in the country. Others simply faded away for reasons best known to them. However, when Prime Minister Dr. Mahathir Mohamad selected Abdullah as his deputy on the 8th of January 1999, the sense of urgency increased. By then, Abdullah was already a major public figure, yet Malaysians knew very little about him. The project ground to a halt, and the search for writers dragged on in the aforementioned manner until the 22nd of June 2002, when Dr. Mahathir surprised the country by announcing his intentions to resign, simultaneously naming Abdullah as his successor. I decided that I had to get the project off the ground once and for all. I once again contacted some of the writers whom I had commissioned earlier. Several said they had become very interested in the project, yet they still could not produce anything substantial.

For a long time now, I have been involved in publishing biographies of outstanding Malaysians. My interest in Malaysian politics and personalities was initially shaped by Malaysia's first Prime Minister, Tunku Abdul Rahman Putra Al-Haj, and the late Tan Sri Mubin Sheppard, both of whom I had the great fortune of getting to know well. Not easily discouraged, I decided that if no one was seriously interested in writing the book, I would attempt to write it myself. After all, I had spent years working with authors in researching and publishing biographies. Before embarking on the project, however, I secured the support of several close friends with regard to my research work, and to assist in my writing skills. The actual writing of the book started in June of 2002 with the first draft completed by the end of 2002.

On the 22nd of August 2002, Abdullah, who was then Deputy Prime Minister, and his charming wife, the endearing Datin Seri Endon Mahmood, were my Guests-of-Honour at the launching of my latest publication, *P. Ramlee: Erti Yang Sakti*, written by Tan Sri Dato' Seri Ahmad Sarji bin Abdul Hamid. At that function, I informed Abdullah of my intention to write a book on him and that I sought his blessings. He intimated to me that if I were to write such a book, its publication should be released only after he had become Prime Minister. Abdullah spent the rest of the evening reminiscing about his childhood and the days when he was in the National Operations Council. I eventually completed the book on Abdullah in the middle of 2003, but postponed its publication.

Now that Abdullah has become Prime Minister, many books have been written on him. If I were to publish the aforementioned completed manuscript which I had written, it would simply be a further duplication of the many books already published on him. My manuscript was not intended to be a comprehensive biography on Abdullah, especially if one uses the criteria that such a biography should describe the subject's entire life, meaning from early childhood through adulthood. Rather, it was intended as a mosaic of my own views based on my research, which relied on information found in the press, magazines and books. I also depended heavily on his speeches, and had interviewed people who were close to him.

I therefore decided to permanently shelve the publication of my manuscript on Abdullah. It was not until recently when I met Dr. Syed Ali Tawfik al-Attas, a close friend and brilliant scholar, while discussing politics and the issue of 'Islam hadhari' with him, that I thought it would be a good idea for him to put his thoughts on the issue in writing. It was then that we decided that part of my manuscript and research could be of use. We decided to extract some of the work from my completed manuscript, complemented with his thoughts, and for the sum total to be published in book form. What you hold before you, *Abdullah Ahmad Badawi:*

Revivalist of an Intellectual Tradition, is the result of this effort.

I wish to mention that my contribution to this book is Chapter One. In addition I contributed to the gathering of certain research materials. The remainder of this book was written entirely by my friend, Dr. Syed Ali Tawfik al-Attas. Although it was my idea to write about Abdullah, it was he who highlighted the importance of defining 'Islam hadhari' in a manner which would lead to intelligible meaning. I thank him for his efforts and suspect that we will be reading more works written by him in future.

In addition, I wish to record my sincere appreciation to Tun Dr. Mahathir Mohamad for giving me the opportunity to be involved in the publication of many of his works over the years, both directly and indirectly. I am greatly honoured and grateful to Dato' Seri Abdullah Haji Ahmad Badawi for his blessings in allowing me to publish this book.

Finally, I wish to mention that without the support and assistance given to us by Dato' Mohamed Abid, the author of *Reflections of Pre-Independence Malaya*, this book would not have been published. He provided several invaluable insights on some of the important political events, and was instrumental in verifying many politically factual details.

Dato' Ng Tieh Chuan
21st January 2005

Prologue

IT IS NOT in my nature to be acutely concerned with super-ficially infallible politically motivated views, especially if those views are concerned with matters of governmental administration and the electoral process. Despite myself, however, recent attempts by the authorities entrusted with administering both the promulgation and definition of the 'concept' of 'Islam hadhari' has challenged me to introduce a preliminary conceptual framework, intended not only as a propaedeutic towards a further elucidation of the afore-mentioned phrase, but more importantly as a scholastic interpretation of what is really meant, in conformity with the intentions of the Prime Minister.

Now that the general scope of the problem addressed in this book has sufficiently been indicated, suffice it to add that attention be directed to the profound importance in consequence of assuming responsibility for precisely explaining the phrase 'Islam hadhari' in a language both lucid and illuminating. With the exception of the Prime Minister's opening remarks concerning the aforementioned subject during the recently concluded UMNO General Assembly, there is as yet no comprehensive work accurately explaining what is meant, consequent to having prior knowledge of the meanings of the individual terms, let alone works offering a plausible definition. Much of what is available on the aforementioned topic is dealt with in an uneven fashion, that is to say, not only do these essays fail to adequately define 'Islam hadhari' in a manner reflective of the worldview of Islām,[1] these works do not consider the etymological aspect of the phrase to adequately describe what is meant, nor make the association between the motives behind this idea and the present state of the Muslims. Subsequent 'definitions' have dealt merely with various aspects of the theme, again without considering the etymological aspect or the relation between this idea and those that preceded it. What is only beginning to be realised, is that in order to sufficiently and adequately explain what is truly meant requires an intellectual understanding of the present situation, in tandem with a profound grasp of the Arabic language, of Islām, the worldview of Islām and its related fundamental elements. Only when this has been

---

[1] There is a distinction to be made here with regard to the phrases 'Islamic worldview' and 'the worldview of Islām'. The former pertains more to the idea of intellectual ideologies or ontological systems conducted under the banner of Islām. These ideologies or ontological systems are then receptive of change. The worldview of Islām however is such that its fundamental elements are immutable because they are based on Revelation.

sufficiently explored and understood should it be possible to envisage a more adequate appreciation of the underlying motives, whose influence on the present age hopes to rival that of the preceding era.

In the meantime, it is my belief that the ideas contained in the following chapters should not be conceived merely as an opinion, but indeed as an intellectually conceived framework derived from direct access to the original source. The ideas complement one another and offer a more complete understanding of the salient features of 'Islam hadhari', and convey intelligible meaning with regard to the blueprint advocated by the Prime Minister.

The purpose of this study, therefore, is an attempt to elucidate one of the more problematic, potentially inflammatory ideological approaches generally ascribed to the prominent leader, statesman, master administrator and political luminary, Abdullah Haji Ahmad Badawi, the fifth Prime Minister of Malaysia, more affectionately referred to simply as 'Pak Lah'. Indeed, one may preface by saying that the poem written by the Prime Minister and introduced at the beginning of this book betrays a certain profound scholarly intellectualism in terms of its subject matter, style and intent. The external interpretation of the aforementioned poetic composition is exceedingly clear; not only does it seek to extol the virtues of integrity and humility, it also seeks to personify responsibility and authority. The internal interpretation is thus the subject matter of this book.

This study follows a deliberate course, one that is intended first to familiarise the reader with key terms and concepts integral to understanding what 'Islam hadhari' is, and how it relates to the Prime Minister's poetic composition. In addition, the intellectual milieu surrounding the Prime Minister, both before he was directly involved in politics and before he was elevated to the highest political office in the country, is weaved into a sketch of his life. Information with regard to his ancestry is largely vacuous. Therefore, we have reconstructed, based largely on reasonable logical deductive methods, what we believe to be a near-accurate depiction of his heritage.

Chapter One, therefore, constitutes a brief biography of the Prime Minister. We have taken liberty not to divulge every detail of his life opting instead to disclose only those features relevant to his current political approach. Chapter Two is concerned with the Prime Minister's heredity. Chapter Three is intended to identify the current predicament of the Muslims. Chapter Four is a brief summary concerned with the rise of philosophy and the sciences according to the framework of the worldview of Islām. Chapter Five constitutes the intellectual milieu prior to al-Ghazzālī, mentioned in the Prime Minister's beautifully penned poetic composition. Chapter Six constitutes the main body of our analysis. Once again, we have taken liberty not to discuss every detail concerned with the phrase 'Islam hadhari', but only as far as it suffices to convey intelligible meaning.

This humble work is the fruit of research done over the past several months at the behest of the Prime Minister. It is, therefore, not only an honour, but incumbent upon me to express my profound gratitude and humble appreciation to our eminent leader, Dato' Seri Abdullah Haji Ahmad

Badawi, Prime Minister of Malaysia. It is to him that I owe the largest portion of gratitude for his friendship, courage, and above all his patience. He has perhaps been the one most eager to see the results of his challenge to me. Several times he expressed interest in the progress of my work; perhaps now, these preliminary remarks will justify that interest.

I am also deeply indebted to Dato' Ng Tieh Chuan, my close friend. It was he who first suggested I put my ideas to paper. Originally he suggested I help him write an addition to the biography of the current Prime Minister, a draft of which he had already completed. Later, I found myself concentrating on elucidating the ideas prevalent to the current administration. I therefore suggested that the book be entitled *Abdullah: Revivalist of an Intellectual Tradition*. We both realised that in doing so, this work would go far beyond the scope of mere biography. His tireless support, commitment and personal encouragement throughout this exercise continues until today. I am indeed honoured that he has allowed our professional relationship to become intertwined in the thicket of friendship.

My admiration is also due to Dato' Mohamed Abid, my cousin and dear friend, for his advice, unceasing support, motivation and personal insights. Without his help and assistance, it is not possible that this project would come to fruition. In addition, I wish to acknowledge the support of my father, Professor Dr. Syed Muhammad Naquib al-Attas, founder and director of the International Institute of Islamic Thought and Civilisation, and holder of the al-Ghazzālī Chair of Islamic Thought. Indeed, under Professor al-Attas' distinguished guidance, the curriculum of the aforementioned Institute was designed to address the needs of present-day Muslims in a manner reflective of what the Prime Minister refers to as 'Islam hadhari'.

I wish to also recognise the assistance and support given to me by my friends and colleagues, Professor Dr. Amer al-Roubaie and Dr. Mesut Idriz in particular. The support of the former was indispensable in allowing me to comprehend and forward the proposals included as part of the epilogue.

Above all, I am eternally indebted to my wife and my children for their undying love, unwavering support, patience, encouragement, and understanding throughout the many trials and tribulations during the most challenging of times. May Allāh continue to shower His blessings upon them and continue to guide them upon the true path which, God willing, will admit them to the ample gardens of His paradise.

Dr. Syed Ali Tawfik al-Attas
21st January 2005

ONE

ABDULLAH AHMAD BADAWI:
ANATOMY OF A POLITICAL CAREER

"I, Abdullah bin Haji Ahmad Badawi, being appointed to hold the office of Prime Minister, do solemnly swear, that I will fulfil the obligations of that post in an honest manner, to the full extent of my capacity, and that I will devote my trust and sincere loyalty to Malaysia, and that I will preserve, protect and defend its Constitution."[1]

WITH THE RECITATION of the aforementioned oath, read together with the oath of secrecy and the signing of the instrument of office before Malaysia's Chief Justice on the 31st of October 2003, Abdullah bin Haji Ahmad Badawi was sworn in as Malaysia's fifth Prime Minister. During the sombre and moving ceremony held at Istana Negara before His Majesty the King, Tuanku Syed Sirajuddin, the nation

---

[1] Translated freely from the Malay language by Syed Ali Tawfik al-Attas.

bore witness to the smooth transition of power which was aired live on television.

Abdullah bin Ahmad Badawi was born on the 26th of November 1939, in Kampung Perlis, Bayan Lepas, in the northern Malaysian state of Penang. He is the eldest of four children of UMNO veteran, Ahmad bin Abdullah (popularly known as Ahmad Badawi), and his wife Kailan binti Haji Hassan. As is the tradition with many Arab and Malay families, Abdullah was named after his grandfather, Abdullah bin Ibrahim (later referred to as Abdullah Fāhim). The latter was a very religious man who had received his tertiary education in Makkah at the blessed Masjid al-Ḥaram under the tutelage of the Imām al-Ḥaramayn. Therefore, naming Abdullah after his grandfather was intended not only for the blessing (*barakah*) associated with his grandfather's name, but it was also intended as a continuation of a legacy. Abdullah was very close to his grandfather, with whom he shared a room when he was growing up. He would be taken by his grandfather to the mosque, erected by the latter, in Kepala Batas to read the Qur'ān while his grandfather would guide him.

His family upbringing was strongly oriented towards Islām because he relied upon his grandfather as his guide throughout his life. According to Abdullah's mother, he has all the characteristics of his grandfather. He even walks and talks like him. His patience and mild demeanour are traits probably inherited from his grandfather. As the eldest son of the family, it was Abdullah's responsibility to look after his younger sister Aminah, and his two brothers, Ibrahim and Mohammad Tahir.

If Abdullah's father, Ahmad Badawi, were alive today, he would most certainly be very proud of his son Abdullah, who not only followed in his footsteps into politics, but went on to become the Prime Minister. Ahmad Badawi was also in Makkah. He followed his parents upon their return to Malaya when he was 10 years old. After completing his primary education in Malaya, he left for Makkah to advance his studies at Makkah al-Mukarramah until he was 30 years old. In 1985 the Arabic language newspaper, *al-Bilād*, published a full page report on the history of football in Saudi Arabia. In that report, Ahmad Badawi was mentioned as being one of the people who had introduced and trained young Arabs in the game of football, and was also among the founders of the football club Malaya Hijaz in Saudi Arabia.

Ahmad Badawi and a few friends had made a pledge while they were in Makkah that they would become involved in politics upon their return to Malaya. The spirit of patriotism among students in Makkah was high at that time. Upon his return to Malaya, he joined the *Persatuan Melayu Seberang Perai* and was duly appointed its chief. In 1946, when UMNO was established by Dato' Onn Ja'afar, he joined and served as UMNO's first Deputy Youth leader, a post he held for 18 years.

Abdullah's father, Ahmad Badawi, was, on two occasions in 1975, acting Chief Minister of Penang during the then Chief Minister's absence. Apart from being the State Executive Councillor and trusted with the portfolio of Islamic Affairs, a post he held from 1972 until 1977, he was also elected Kepala Batas assemblyman for three terms—

1959, 1964 and 1969. During his appointment as State Executive Councillor, he was also an assemblyman for Bertam between 1974 and 1977.

For all those years as an assemblyman, and even as acting Chief Minister, Ahmad Badawi only accepted the fixed monthly allowance due to him. He never made any other claims even though he was entitled to do so. When asked about this, he said that the fixed allowance was enough for him. As the principal of the *Dā'irat al-Ma'ārif al-Wataniyyah*, he only received a meagre salary.[2] Ahmad Badawi passed away on the 8th of May 1977 at the age of 72.

It was raining when Abdullah finally arrived home after being sworn in as Malaysia's fifth Prime Minister. Apart from his wife Endon, his mother, Kailan binti Haji Hassan had been his pillar of strength. He went straight to his mother, knelt at her feet and kissed her hand. In the evening, he broke fast with her and other family members and then joined the rest of the village folk who had gathered at his home to perform evening prayers.

In his early youth, Abdullah was educated at Sekolah Kebangsaan Permatang Bertam until standard four, and subsequently pursued his studies at a special Malay class which was established by the British Government for Malay students who excelled in their primary school studies at Bukit Mertajam High School in Province Wellesley. He later continued his post secondary education at the Methodist

---

[2] Mokhtar Petah, *Abdullah Badawi—Pejuang Kemanusian Sejagat* (Kuala Lumpur: Pustaka Antara Sdn. Bhd., 1997).

Boys School in Penang. While in secondary school, he also attended religious classes in the afternoon at the *Dā'irat al-Ma'ārif al-Waṭaniyyah*, the religious school founded by his grandfather. Today, the school is well known for having produced many outstanding religious scholars (*'ulamā'*) over several decades, including State official expounder's of Islamic law (*muftī*). Today, Abdullah is the school's patron.

As a young boy, Abdullah would follow his father to political functions and rallies. One such event that made a permanent impact on him was in 1948 when he first saw Dato' Onn bin Ja'afar, the founder of UMNO. During an interview, in the presence of Mohamed Abid and me at his residence in 2003, he fondly recalled the event in 1948 when he saw Dato' Onn:

"I saw Dato' Onn in the year 1948, when he was in Butterworth. He was there presiding over an UMNO Youth parade of 15,000 youths, dressed in white; white shirts, white trousers and *songkok*. And I remember Dato' Onn was so impressive. I didn't understand much of what he was saying—I was only a 10-year-old boy—but I could recognise, I could know in my heart that he was a great leader because when he spoke, people were clapping again, again and again. And there must be something great about this man. My father then was the Parade Commander of UMNO Youth, and later on I remembered my father said he was so impressed with the UMNO Youth. They were so disciplined. He said the only thing lacking was that they didn't have a gun in their hands. But later I knew that Sir Gerald Templer was not happy about UMNO Youth having uniforms of white shirts and white trousers and *songkok*. So the uniform was banned. So that was the story of UMNO Youth. Anyway, certainly Dato' Onn was a very inspiring leader. He spoke well in English and Malay, yet made selfless sacrifices in order to save his people. The Malays are his people. He belonged to the Malay race and he did what he could. Dato' Onn was our hero. He was a great leader. He was able to unite the Malays throughout the Peninsula, to fight for independence. Therefore, my belief is that no history book of Malaysia, of modern Malaysia, can be written without including in it a story of Dato' Onn and his selfless struggle to unite the Malays to oppose the British, because of the proposal in setting up the Malayan Union, later on uniting them to fight for independence. Dato' Onn made the greatest contribution by assuring that all the Malays were united and could identify themselves as Malays, not as orang Johor, orang Kelantan, orang Kedah or orang Penang, no more, but as Malays. And they are known as Malays and united in a new party which he set up, and that is UMNO. Without UMNO there would be no 'Alliance', there would be no Tunku Abdul Rahman as we know him. Without the alliance of UMNO, MCA and MIC, there would be no Independence. Therefore, the present generation must be grateful to Dato' Onn for having sowed the first seeds for the struggle of our independence."[3]

It is worth noting that despite his strong religious background, Abdullah had a secular education. It is clear that the

---

[3] Interview with Abdullah for a video clip screened at the launching of the book, *Reflections of Pre-Independence Malaya*.

experiences gained during this period had an important multicultural impact on him.

While waiting for his High School Certificate results, Abdullah got involved in student and political activism. Even then, his leadership skills were apparent. While in school, he represented the Malay Student's Association of Pulau Pinang and Seberang Perai as a delegate to the annual congress of the *Malay Students Association of the Peninsula* (GPMS). This was in 1957 while only in Form Five. Among the initiatives he started were tuition classes to help Malay students in their studies. According to a friend, Ahmad Subky, at that time Abdullah was known as 'the Father of Tuition Classes'.[4] Meanwhile, he won a Malaysian Civil Service scholarship to read economics, but he decided to follow in his grandfather's and father's footsteps by choosing Islamic studies for his honours course. Abdullah was accepted to the University of Malaya as an undergraduate, at which time he tendered his membership in the *Malay Students Association of the Peninsula*. This marked the beginning of his long involvement with the association, a relationship which saw him become President of the association from 1961 until 1964. Today he remains as its advisor. In 1964, Abdullah graduated with honours from the University of Malaya with a Bachelor of Arts degree majoring in Islamic studies.

After graduating in 1964 from the University of Malaya, Abdullah followed the example of many of his Malay contemporaries and began his career in the Malaysian Civil

---

[4] *Bapa Kelas Bimbingan* in the Malay language.

Service (MCS). Abdullah's first appointment in the civil service was as Assistant Secretary in the Federal Establishment Office.[5] In the civil service, his superiors soon recognised his administrative abilities, and in mid-1969 he was appointed Principal Assistant Secretary to the newly established National Operations Council (NOC). This turned out to be an important milestone in Abdullah's career because the Government, and the country, was still reeling from the unprecedented and totally unexpected events associated with the 13th of May 1969 racial riots. In this key position under the dynamic leadership of Abdul Razak Hussein, who later became the second Prime Minister, Abdullah had to oversee the work of the Council that literally involved 'picking up the pieces', towards building a new concept for a multiracial society. The Council faced a formidable task because it had to work closely with individuals and groups representing a cross-section of the society, many of whom were, in fact, directly or indirectly traumatised by the effects of the riots. He therefore had to work hard to bridge the racial divide between the nation's Malay, Chinese and Indian communities, particularly when it came to the different religious groups involved.

In 1965, Abdullah joined UMNO as an ordinary member.[6] In the early 1970's, the UMNO leadership published a book entitled *Revolusi Mental*, which was under the patronage of UMNO's former Secretary-General, Senu Abdul

---

[5] Now known as the Public Services Department.
[6] It was also in this year, on the 4th of September 1965, Abdullah married Endon, one of 11 siblings of Dato' Mahmood Ambak and Datin Mariam Abdullah, the latter an amicable Japanese native.

Rahman. Abdullah was the coordinating editor for the book. Unfortunately, the book was not published with the names of the contributors preceding each chapter. Some would later say that the book presented an image of the Malays as an inherently backward, ill-educated and miserable race, trapped in a dark world of superstition with a blind deference to authority and lack of economic sense. An extract from the introduction to the English translation[7] of the book reads:

> "*Revolusi Mental* is a movement for change. It is aimed at moving and shaking every part of the Malay community, with no exception. This vital change in the Malay community will give security and integrity to Malaysian society as a whole. Without this change, Malaysian society will remain vulnerable. This is also an answer for non-Malays who have been seeing the Malays as dependent on government help and reluctant to work on their own as the other communities do. Hence, we believe that this movement will not cause anxiety or be misunderstood as being racist, especially today when Malaysia is resounding with calls towards goodwill and solidarity. This revolution is different from the political or social revolutions that have taken place in some countries. This revolution does not demand sacrifices in the form of bloodshed or property loss. This revolution is not directed against any individual, group or notion, but at the Malays themselves; it is

---

[7]   Senu Abdul Rahman ed., *Revolusi Mental* (Kuala Lumpur: United Malays National Organisation, 1971). The book has been translated from Malay into English by Adibah Amin. The English edition is entitled *Mental Revolution* (Petaling Jaya: Pelanduk Publications, 2004.)

introverted, not extroverted. In short, this is a revolution of looking inwards, probing deep into the Malay mind. The decision to launch this revolution is based on a study of the weaknesses of the Malays in all fields. Some non-Malays in this country also agree that a radical, revolutionary change must occur in the Malay way of thinking. We are confident, therefore, that by promoting the 'revolusi mental' concept, we will not cause any individuals or groups to feel threatened or to think that this movement is meant to undermine their position or security. We present this book [*Revolusi Mental*] to the reader as a first effort in the 'revolusi mental' (mental revolution) movement."[8]

It is therefore not surprising, that Abdullah himself acknowledged his involvement in the National Operations Council as being an education. "We were a nation looking for a new foundation; people spoke their minds and there were all these inspiring ideas". Indeed, considering that the genesis of the concept of a united front first envisioned by the founder of UMNO and later realised with the formation of the Barisan Nasional[9] may be traced to this period, it is altogether plausible that his involvement with the Council helped him realise his own potential in contributing towards the building of a multiracial, multicultural Malaysia.

The next step in Abdullah's career came in 1971, when Tun Abdul Razak promoted him to a new appointment as Director of Youth at the Ministry of Culture, Youth and

---

[8] Senu Abdul Rahman, *Revolusi Mental* (Kuala Lumpur: United Malays National Organisation, 1971).

[9] Or United Front.

Sports after the National Operations Council had wound up. Tun Abdul Razak wanted the youth of Malaysia to be mobilised for the development of future Malaysia. In 1974, he became the Ministry's Deputy Secretary-General. His role in the Ministry gave him the opportunity to be involved in the planning and implementation of programmes and projects in keeping with the objectives of the NOC in finding ways to strengthen national unity. He was also instrumental in setting up the National Youth Consultative Council and represented the government in interacting with the country's youth leaders. Among the urgent tasks that he had to address were issues related to the use of Malay as the national language, the Societies Act, the Internal Security Act, education, poverty in the rural areas, religion, youth training and development programmes.

The year 1977 was an important turning point for Abdullah. That same year, on the 8th of May, his father passed away. Abdullah was urged by both family and friends, who included several UMNO members in his native State of Penang, to take his father's place when the by-election for the state constituency of Bertam was held. Abdullah finally acquiesced, but was asked to postpone his intentions because his services were still required at the national level.

UMNO veteran, Dato' Md. Noor Ahmad, recounts the early days when it took him four months to persuade Abdullah to quit the civil service and become a full-time politician. It began in late 1977, when Dato' Md. Noor received a call from the office of Tun Hussein Onn, Malaysia's third Prime Minister, asking him to nominate two candidates for the Kepala Batas Parliamentary seat. "I was told the Prime Minister wanted to call for the General Election in 1978 and wanted to inject new blood into Barisan Nasional. He wanted to strengthen the coalition and specifically mentioned Kepala Batas as one of the seats that should have a younger representative", recalls Dato' Md. Noor. A former three-term assemblyman himself, Dato' Md. Noor said two names came to his mind; Abdullah, who was then the Deputy Secretary-General to the Ministry of Culture, Youth and Sports; and former Education Ministry Director-General, Tan Sri Murad Md. Noor, also a Penang native. He immediately went to Kuala Lumpur to meet the two men who both rejected the idea outright. "It was like playing ping-pong. Abdullah asked me to persuade Murad, and Murad asked me to refer the matter to Abdullah. I did not give up. I went to see them again twice. At the last meeting, Murad told me that politics was not his strength. He told me that the government could use his expertise in education, whereas Abdullah had the political background because both his father and grandfather were active in UMNO".[10] Dato' Md. Noor subsequently went to see Abdullah for the fourth time at his office in early 1978 and relayed what Murad had said. Abdullah, he recalled, looked straight at him and said that he would consider the idea, adding, *"Biarlah saya sembahyang istikharah dahulu"*.[11]

---

[10] See Dato' Md. Noor Ahmad's interview with *The Star*, 1st November 2003.

[11] Freely translated as, "Allow me to first perform prayers seeking divine help".

When general elections were held in 1978, Abdullah was nominated by UMNO to contest the Kepala Batas parliamentary seat. He went on to win the Kepala Batas parliamentary seat, defeating rival candidate Haji Musa Mohd. Yatim of PAS, by a convincing majority of 5,029 votes and was appointed parliamentary secretary of the Federal Territory Ministry. In December of that year, he became Deputy Head of the Penang UMNO liaison committee. Soon afterwards, he was also elected Head of the UMNO division of Kepala Batas.

In the following years, Abdullah's rise through both the government and party ranks was meteoric. His first position in national politics was as Parliamentary Secretary to the Federal Territory Ministry in July of 1978. On the 16th of September 1980, he was promoted to Deputy Federal Territory Minister. His rise in Government also began to garner the attention of UMNO members and, in June of 1981, he was elected to the UMNO Supreme Council. This signalled the arrival of another rising star within UMNO, because former Prime Minister, Tun Dr. Mahathir Mohamad, soon after assuming office in July of 1981, named Abdullah as Minister in the Prime Minister's Department, a clear sign that Abdullah was being groomed for even greater responsibilities.

Thereafter, Abdullah's political fortunes seemed almost unstoppable. In May of 1984, he was elected one of three vice-presidents of UMNO and on the 14th of July that same year, he was appointed Minister of Education. As Minister of Education, Abdullah strongly advocated a policy aimed at urging Malays to pursue science and technology through the

Joint-Secretariat on Scholarships Abroad. As a result, an estimated 25,000 Malay students with good grades were progressively sent to pursue academic studies in the United States of America and the United Kingdom. He represented Malaysia in the Islamic Scientific, Education, Social and Cultural Organisation (ISESCO), which is the Islamic equivalent of UNESCO.

Abdullah was also responsible for the formulation of the National Book Policy, which was approved by the Cabinet on the 27th of November 1985. The policy aimed to ensure an integrated book development in Malaysia. The Cabinet also approved the setting-up of a committee comprising the relevant government agencies to ensure a smooth implementation of the policy. According to a publication released by the National Book Council of Malaysia:

> "The National Book Policy has four important objectives. First, to ensure that books in Malay will play an effective role as a tool for intellectual, social and cultural development, in line with the needs and aspirations of the country. Second, to ensure that books could be enjoyed by all levels of society. Third, to ensure that all citizens in the country developed an interest in reading so that by the year 2020, Malaysian society can be said to be a reading society; and fourth, to ensure that all books published in the country are of high quality, not only in terms of contents, but also in their physical form. To achieve those aims the nation must ensure that all activities pertaining to the publication of books must be accepted as a part of the education industry, and as such must be incorporated into the development

plans of the country. A special allocation should be embarked for the development of books. The nation must also ensure that the book industry is recognised as one of the essential industries, i.e. a very vital cultural activity."[12]

It indicated that the book industry would not be able to progress if conditions were not conductive to its development. The National Book Policy:

"... outlines seven factors that are necessary for the development of books: 1. High literacy rate and widespread interest in reading; 2. Recognition of the book industry as an important cultural industry; 3. Economic conditions that could help the book Industry; 4. Effective promotion, distribution and selling of books; 5. A complete chain of libraries that can help books reach their readers; 6. A national education system that requires books to educate and develop the thinking of young generations in pursuing knowledge; 7. A language policy that should not hinder reading."[13]

The National Book Policy further suggested seven plans of action, namely,

"The implementation of the Reading Movement Project in earnest, develop local writers; develop translators, set up a school of publishing; recognise production of books as an important industry in the

---

[12] The National Book Council of Malaysia, *National Book Policy* (Kuala Lumpur: Dewan Bahasa dan Pustaka, 1992).
[13] Ibid.

country; carry out concerted actions on the promotion, distribution and sale of books, build an integrated plan for the expansion of libraries, and establish a professional body that carries out functions for the development of books."[14]

Abdullah served as Minister of Education until 1986, at which time he was appointed Minister of Defence. Abdullah's political fortunes changed completely on the 24th of April 1987. He had supported a group of UMNO leaders led by Tengku Razaleigh Hamzah, who were opposed to the leadership of Dr. Mahathir. As a result of this decision, Abdullah spent the next three years and nine months in the 'political wilderness', a period he would later describe as, "my sabbatical leave". Tengku Razaleigh had formed an alliance with former Deputy Prime Minister Dato' Musa Hitam, whose purpose was to challenge Dr. Mahathir at the party elections which were held in April of 1987. Although former rivals, Abdullah and Tengku Razaleigh resolved to overcome their differences in order to present a united front against the leadership of Dr. Mahathir. For his part, Dr. Mahathir teamed up with former Deputy Prime Minister and UMNO veteran, Tun Abdul Ghafar Baba. The bitter campaign resulted in a narrow win for UMNO President and Deputy-President, in favour of both Dr. Mahathir and Abdul Ghafar Baba respectively. However, despite having supported candidates opposed to the leadership of Dr. Mahathir, Abdullah managed to emerge second, thus retaining his vice-presidential position.

---

[14] Ibid.

Having secured his position in UMNO, Dr. Mahathir started purging the Cabinet of all his political opponents, which included Abdullah. Despite his position as an UMNO Vice-President, Abdullah found himself ostracised from the government and was subsequently dispatched to the political wilderness. Some have said that the political purge was surprising, especially since it came on the very first day of Ramadan. Many expected a forgiving nature since Ramadan was the fasting month, the month of forgiveness.

Some of Dr. Mahathir's supporters were taken aback by the dismissal of Abdullah. After all, Abdullah had won the vice-president's post with the second highest number of votes in the party election. Dr. Mahathir's subsequent political purge was regarded as a clear indication that there would be no spirit of consensus, nor would there be any accommodation given to his political opponents.

Many believed that Abdullah's political career was over the day he was relieved of his post as Defence Minister. It was the 7th of May 1987. Many did not even devote any time to him, refusing to even greet him. Unfortunately, Abdullah was seen as someone who could sully the reputation of anyone associated with him. Surprisingly, he was still 'Mr Nice Guy', but the varnish of his carefully lacquered image had grown dull, and as a result, those professing friendship in the beginning now began to tire of him.

Abdullah's late mother said in an interview, that she would never forget the day her eldest son, Abdullah, returned to their hometown in Kepala Batas alone by taxi after he was dropped as Defence Minister in the Cabinet reshuffle of 1987. "It was so sad suddenly to see him alone without his usual escorts. Even some of his colleagues had ditched him. At that time, I thought his political career was over".[15]

"At that time, I could not bear to see him suffer. I felt so sorry for him. Time and again, I would tell him that Allāh will always be with those who are patient and resilient. As a mother, my prayers will always be with him and I also told him to leave everything to God. We have to believe in Qada and Qadar. We propose, God disposes. We cannot fight against fate. I also told him not to change but to keep with his good traits should he find success in future".[16]

Her advice has helped Abdullah weather the ups and downs in his political career, particularly during the period of his self proclaimed 'sabbatical leave'.

Despite this serious setback, Abdullah did not want to establish a rival political party. He refused to leave UMNO and worked hard to help heal the split that had developed within the Organisation's rank and file, fearing that if UMNO were to suffer a division, the consequences would be irreversible. To this end, he travelled around the country to meet UMNO members, even though he was not always welcomed. But he was not discouraged. When asked about the years in the political wilderness, Abdullah says;

---

[15] Saiful Azhar Abdullah, "A Natural Successor", *New Straits Times*, 1st November 2003.
[16] Datuk Kailan Hassan's interview with *The Star*, 1st November 2003.

"I don't know if it is political wilderness. Some people say it is. But during those three years and nine months, I was still party Vice-President. I was asked to be the leader of the UMNO delegation to MAPEN-I (the National Economic Consultative Council) and we spent about two years. I was engaged with the work of MAPEN, and there were so many discussions. I kept myself very busy. I could not devote a lot of attention to anything else other than politics, and to visiting places. During that period, I do not remember having had any quarrels with him [Dr. Mahathir]. I saw the difficulties. I saw hurdles in front of me but I was determined to stay in the party. I have never been in Semangat 46. I have been with UMNO all the time. I can continue to make my contribution and I believe in doing that. I always believe that one can continue if one feels that they have something to contribute. One can contribute in many ways, whether one is in the government or out. And that was what I did. I continued to work hard. I showed that I remained committed to UMNO's struggle, and to the Barisan Nasional. I have always been present, and I have spent a lot of time whenever there was a by-election because others are too busy. So that was what I did. I maintained my presence in UMNO although not in the government, and not in the Cabinet".[17]

I was introduced to Dato' Mohamed Abid[18] by Abdullah. The former, is one of a handful of friends who stood by him

---

[17] Interview with *The Star*, 1st November 2003.

[18] Dato' Mohamed Abid is the author of *Reflections of Pre-Independence Malaya* (Petaling Jaya: Pelanduk Publications, 2003).

during the difficult period of his political life. Mohamed Abid refers to this period as 'the dark age' of Abdullah's political career. Mohamed Abid and his wife Marina Kamaliah Anwar were so close to Abdullah's family that in 1995, when their daughter, Mastisa Hani, married Mokhzani Mahathir, Dr. Mahathir's son, they surprised their guests by asking Abdullah to deliver the customary thank-you speech on their behalf. According to Mohamed Abid:

"The sad part was when he was not in the government because he was abandoned by many of his former colleagues and friends. He had only a few loyal friends. One of them was the late Dato' Abdul Fatah Abdullah, who was also his former political secretary. They would often play golf at the Royal Selangor Golf Club and have family dinners at each other's house, at or the house of another good friend. They would go on trips to visit their children who were studying in London where they would spend time walking and window shopping because they didn't have the money to buy things. During that period, Abdullah had to sell two of his houses. His only income then was his Cabinet pension, and allowance from working with the National Economic Consultative Council (MAPEN).Having lost his job in Dr. Mahathir's Cabinet, Abdullah also lost all the benefits and privileges of power as a Minister. He was suddenly without an office where he could meet his friends and UMNO members from his constituency. He then decided to set up his office with the help of his best friend, the late Dato' Abdul Fatah Abdullah on the 11th Floor of the Pernas Building in Jalan Raja Laut, Kuala Lumpur, where his sister-in-law, Noor Asiah, who manages a travel agency, gave him two rooms. But many of his friends and UMNO members were afraid that people would know that they were visiting him".[19]

According to Dato' Wong Chun Wai:

"Not wanting to be noticed entering Abdullah's office, some timid party members had used the elevator which stopped at Bank Islam, before using the staircase to walk up to his office. A simple man who prefers cobbling together a consensus to confronting his foes, the erudite politician is known for his accessibility to the grassroots. Because of his unwillingness to be combative, he has been regarded as soft and overly cautious by some, but that is because they have not seen the other side of him— his unwavering stand on matters of principle. The press sometimes feels that he does not make a good copy because he is not known for being rhetorical or sensational, preferring to make careful statements. But it is hard to find fault with Abdullah. A pious person who leads a simple lifestyle, the 'Mr. Clean' image fits him well. Pak Lah [Abdullah], as he is affectionately known, is also a forgiving man. He understood the predicament of certain UMNO members who were reluctant to be seen with him when he was in the political wilderness,"[20]

---

[19] See *The Star*, 1st November 2003.
[20] See *The Star*, 1st November 2003.

Mohamed Abid remembers that:

"It was around this time that Abdullah was often seen lunching at 'Santa's Chapathi House', a worn-out plasterboard shop which seduces customers with its mouth-watering aroma, just behind Jalan Tuanku Abdul Rahman. This was one of Abdullah's favourite shops. It was also closest to his office. But because there was no air-conditioning, one or two of his friends would go down first to order the food. When the *chapathi* was ready, they would call him. The heat was so oppressive that no one it seemed, could last more than 30 minutes in the shop. Everyone, including Abdullah, would eat quickly when the food was laid on the table. He is a very God-fearing family man, very humble and pragmatic and his advice would always be, "be patient" because he always says that at the end of the day, those who are patient will be rewarded. I have never heard him bad-mouthing anyone, including those who did not like him. I believe this has got to do with his strong religious background and upbringing. People always call him 'Mr. Nice Guy' and some say that he is soft Please don't underestimate him, he can be very tough and firm, if the situation warrants. During the 1990 party election when the results were broadcast, the news announced that he had won one of the vice-president's posts. He immediately called my daughter from his home in Bangsar. Abdullah thanked her because she had fasted and prayed for three days for his victory. He never forgot those delegates who supported him because if they had not, he would not be here today. He won the party election in 1990 with the second highest votes as

Vice-President, and because of the result, the Prime Minister decided to appoint him as Minister again. That is a reflection of his character—a man who is humble, kind and appreciative."[21]

Once, just before the 1990 UMNO election, Abdullah, perhaps in a moment of uncertainty, said to Mohamed Abid, "if I fail this time, shall we go into business together?" Mohamed Abid laughed and replied, "just concentrate on politics, you know nothing about business".[22]

In 1990, despite having no government position, the UMNO General Assembly re-elected Abdullah as one of the party's three Vice-Presidents with the second highest number of votes. Accordingly, in March of 1991, Dr. Mahathir appointed him Minister of Foreign Affairs. His loyalty to UMNO, by refusing to join the rival political party, and his continued efforts in strengthening UMNO outside his native State in spite of his political isolation, did not go unnoticed. His religious background and reputation as the incorruptible 'Mr. Clean' was enough to convince Dr. Mahathir to re-instate him. According to Mohamed Abid, "it is very hard to bring down someone like Abdullah, because he doesn't have skeletons in his closet, or is the subject of scandal". At the close of the 1990 general election, Mohamed Abid went along with Abdullah as he went to cast his vote in Kepala Batas. Before they reached the Barisan Nasional booth, Abdullah stopped to greet the opposition at a PAS polling

---

[21] See *The Star*, 1st November 2003.

[22] See the article, "Just Reward for Mr. Nice Guy", by Rose Ismail, *New Straits Times*, 1st November 2003.

station. As they left, Mohamed Abid overheard one manning the booth lamenting, "if this is the way he (Abdullah) behaves towards us, we will surely lose today". To his detractors, the fact that Abdullah had lost the Vice-Presidential post in 1993 was viewed as 'the beginning of the end' because even though he was retained as Minister of Foreign Affairs, that portfolio was not of any benefit for an ambitious politician.

Unlike the other appointments Abdullah held in the Ministries of Defence and Education, the Ministry of Foreign Affairs has rarely been regarded as being one particularly desirable to ambitious political leaders anxious to establish a personal power base. It seemed to many that the aforementioned post would be a handicap for Abdullah, as it would deprive him of precious time and opportunity to meet with party members at the grassroots. However, political observers noted that Abdullah seemed quite content with his position, in spite of the fact that Dr. Mahathir's strong interest in foreign affairs often meant that Abdullah would assume a back seat. However, he settled well into his job as Minister of Foreign Affairs and soon established himself as one of the most respected Foreign Ministers the country has ever had. Abdullah—always a team player—was content to work behind the scenes. Even so, his contribution to strengthening political and economic ties with members of the Association of Southeast Asian Nations (ASEAN) during this period was particularly significant.

On the 10th of February 1991, a major Cabinet reshuffle was announced. What resulted was the appointment of Abdullah as Minister of Foreign Affairs, which took effect on the 15th of March that same year. The appointment came "like a bolt of lightning, out of the blue" Abdullah told reporters. "I am touched and shocked to hear the announcement ... but I am grateful to the Prime Minister for having the trust to allow me to serve again. I will continue to work and serve the nation and its people," he said at UMNO's headquarters in Kuala Lumpur.

Abdullah was appointed Foreign Minister towards the end of the Gulf War. It was a trying period where Abdullah was faced with several complex issues, including the controversy over the East Asia Economic Caucus and the overlapping claims on the issue of the Spratly Islands, Gulf War issues notwithstanding. Other issues which required deft decision-making was called for, including ASEAN and the Bosnia-Herzegovina episode. Fortunately, Abdullah adapted well. Some have argued that Dr. Mahathir's prominence in international affairs made Abdullah's job easier. With Dr. Mahathir setting the pace, all that Abdullah and Wisma Putra, or the Ministry of Foreign Affairs, had to do was to follow up on the finer details. The reality, however, was somewhat different. Not only had the end of the Cold War given rise to a new set of complications, international relations had come to be intricately linked to economic development, trade and investment. Abdullah did not simply wait for Dr. Mahathir to take the lead, he was responsible for a myriad of new initiatives himself.

As Foreign Minister, Abdullah represented Malaysia with distinction. However, the appointment soon took its toll. The last quarter of 1995 was a particularly busy period. There were a string of back-to-back meetings and assignments; the General Assembly in New York, an official visit to Washington, DC, the Non-Aligned Movement Summit in Cartegena, the special session commemorating the United Nations' 50th anniversary in New York, a working visit to London, then to Buenos Aires for a G15 meeting, followed by a trip to Auckland for the Commonwealth Heads of Government Meeting, Osaka for the Asia Pacific Economic Cooperation, on to London for a conference on the Dayton Peace Plan, finally terminating in Bangkok for the ASEAN Summit.

At the end of it all, after he had traversed more time zones than he would care to remember, Abdullah took a week's break. His wife insisted that he go for a medical check-up at the National Heart Institute. Following her advice, he was told he had one blocked artery and another which was dangerously narrow. Although he had not experienced any angina or breathlessness, doctors insisted an operation was necessary. Open-heart surgery was performed on the 15th of January 1996.

The operation prompted many observers to write Abdullah off politically, suggesting in particular that he may be too ill to contest the UMNO Vice-Presidency during the UMNO General Assembly of 1996. In typical fashion, Abdullah brushed such suggestions aside. "I do not intend to change the decision I have made to offer myself as a Vice-President" he told the press. "Thank God ... after the treatment at the National Heart Institute, I feel healthier". He subsequently garnered 1,053 votes at the party Assembly, securing second place for himself from amongst the seven contenders for the three vice-presidential positions. The election effectively restored him to the position he lost in 1993.

As Foreign Minister for close to eight years, Abdullah had become a familiar face on the international stage. The goodwill that he had nurtured and the friendships that he had forged would now be of use for the task that was ahead as Prime Minister. As Minister of Foreign Affairs, he had performed exceptionally well and proved his mettle to his detractors, who assumed that his appointment as Minister of Foreign Affairs marked 'the beginning of the end'. He persevered to become the fifth Prime Minister of Malaysia and President of UMNO.

TWO

ABDULLAH FĀHIM[1]

THE STORY OF Abdullah Haji Ahmad Badawi would not be complete without considering the role of his grandfather, Abdullah Fāhim. Since the former is said to possess some of the more virtuous characteristics of his grandfather, it is necessary for us to offer a brief summary of him. In order to do so, one must first examine his family tree (*shajarah*). This in itself, however, poses several difficulties. To begin with, there is no written family tree, so therefore, any

[1] In order to construct a plausible history of the Prime Minister's family, both Dr. Mesut Idriz and I travelled to Kepala Batas, Penang, on Sunday, the 15th of August 2004, to meet with and interview former member of Penang's State Legislative Council and UMNO Secretary for Kepala Batas, Dato' Haji Mohd. Noor Ahmad, and Dato' Haji Arshad Haji Zakaria, Congregation Chairman of Masjid *al-Jāmi' al-Badawī* in Kepala Batas. We wish to thank them both for their cooperation, assistance and hospitality during our visit.

reference made to his ancestral lineage relies upon word of mouth transmission. Herein lies another problem. Verbal transmission relies upon several factors. To begin with, the transmitter must be one whose character cannot be the subject of doubt. In addition, his recollection relies upon his memory. Since what he relates was not recorded, his mental recollection cannot be confirmed except by another who has either witnessed those recollections firsthand, or whose character is not subject to doubt. Factual information about the ancestral lineage of Abdullah Haji Ahmad Badawi is extremely scarce; the only somewhat reliable information about his ancestral lineage comes from Abdullah himself, the contemporaries of his father, Ahmad, and from the students of his grandfather, Abdullah Fāhim. All additional information with regard to his ancestral lineage is then only speculative in nature, although we have, wherever possible, logically deduced some remarks.

It is often assumed that Abdullah Haji Ahmad Badawi's descent originates in Arabia. Some may even claim that his descent originates in Morocco, North Africa. As we shall see however, with reference to the latter statement, this is a little misleading since Muslim descent is traditionally patriarchal, in other words, descent follows from the male side of the family. Unfortunately, information with regard to the male ancestry of Abdullah Haji Ahmad Badawi is largely vacuous. This fact notwithstanding, for the purpose of this book, we have explored the possibility of Abdullah's North African lineage because we believe both claims, in other words, the North African and the Arabian aspect, are vital in constructing a plausible explanation with regard to his intellectual heritage.

In reference to the possibility of Abdullah's descent from North Africa, it all began with a man named Abdul Kadir. Apparently he migrated from Morocco to what was then the kingdom of Siam and wed a native whose name is not at our disposal. The couple had a son named Muhammad who later became the congregational prayer leader (*imām*) of a mosque in a village named Setul, in southern Siam. Muhammad had a son named Alang Kecil who was wed to Fatimah. They were blessed with four offspring—Saiyah, Muhammad Saman, Zainab and Hamidah. The latter was married to a man named Saleh and the couple was bestowed with three children—Khatijah, Aminah and Muhammad Yatim. The eldest, Khatijah, later wed a man named Ibrahim and were in turn blessed with four offspring of their own—Tahir, Abdullah, Kalsom and Asma. Abdullah, who later came to be known as Abdullah Fāhim, had four offspring of his own—Khadijah, Ghazali, Ahmad and Abdul Hamid. Ahmad, who later came to be referred to as Ahmad Badawi, was the current Prime Minister's father.

Traditionally, those who originate from Arab lands have long names indicating who their forefathers were, and perhaps a surname indicative of their profession, or of their country or village of birth, or both. For instance, Ḥujjat al-Islām Abū Hāmid Muḥammad ibn Muhammad ibn Muhammad al-Ghazzālī al-Tūsī (450-505H/1058-1111CE). Hujjat al-Islām, meaning 'the proof of Islām', is an honorific title bestowed upon al-Ghazzālī during his lifetime, not simply by virtue of his piety but also by virtue of his intellectual contribution towards defending and explaining the religion of Islām in a manner unsurpassed by any, both prior to and consequent to his appearance in the intellectual milieu of Muslim scholarship and learning. Abū Ḥāmid, or 'father of Ḥāmid', denotes his nickname (*kunyah*). Then comes his name, Muhammad, followed by both his father's and grandfather's name. This is then followed by his family name (*laqab*) indicated by the name Ghazzālī, which is preceded by the definite article 'al'. Al-Ghazzālī therefore means 'one who is a spinner of yarn', perhaps to denote the occupation of the ancestral family of al-Ghazzālī. Finally, the name terminates with the denotation al-Ṭūsī, given to indicate the place of origin, in this case the city of Ṭūs in Persia.

It is apparent from the aforementioned brief ancestral sketch pertaining to Abdullah Haji Ahmad Badawi's lineage that this tradition is absent. Does this therefore mean that the subject, namely Abdul Kadir, did not originate from the Arab world? On the contrary, it could simply mean that the scribe entrusted with preparing the sketch either did not have any reliable information with regard to his subject, or that he simply ignored tradition. Another point worthy of mention has to do with the spelling of the subject's name. If he had indeed hailed from the Arab world, would not his name be spelled in the following manner, 'Abd al-Qādir? Once again we will reply that the spelling of the subject's name does not hold any major significance. Since this is perhaps the first time anyone is making a reasonable attempt to construct a plausible account of the Prime Minister's ancestral lineage, the names of his forefather's have been spelled in accordance with the local vernacular.[2]

We are of the opinion that Abdul Kadir was a Muslim missionary. It is an undisputed fact that Muslim missionaries and traders from the Arab world came to the Malay archipelago on ships. It is also an undisputed fact that many of these missionaries conducted religious classes for the benefit of the local populace. It is also possible that these missionaries would select some of their more brilliant students to accompany them back to the Arab world where their intellectual journey could continue. In fact, many mystic's (*sūfī's*) from the Malay world travelled to the Arab world to refine their knowledge of the Quranic sciences and the *hadīth* (narratives of the Prophet). In addition, it is also true that many missionaries would often settle in lands they had come to propagate the teachings of Islām, often times giving references to their students who would then travel to the Arab world to further their education under another master or tutor.

In Abdul Kadir's case this is perhaps true. As a missionary he travelled to the kingdom of Siam where he wed a local native and started teaching. But is it not the case that missionaries generally establish a religious brotherhood (*tarīqah*) punctuated by a school of thought or a style of dress which would identify them as belonging to that

---

[2] One is not suggesting that the correct name of the Prime Minister's ancestor would read 'Abd al-Qādir al-Maghribī, because at that time we are not even sure if a country called 'al-Maghrib' even existed. Furthermore traditionally, Arab surnames adopted the names of their tribes, or the names of their birthplace.

religious brotherhood? We will say that this is generally not the case. No doubt some missionaries did indeed establish religious brotherhoods (*turuq*), but these were either punctuated by an outstanding contribution to the tradition of scholarship and learning, or were marked by extreme ideologies which were deemed unacceptable to the majority of Muslims. In general however, these missionaries commanded students and followers without deeming it necessary to be identified by a particular religious brotherhood.

If one is to assume that there is a possibility that the Prime Minister's ancestral lineage is inextricably linked to North Africa, then it is very possible that Abdul Kadir originated from Marakkesh, one of the more identifiable centres of learning in Morocco, and then travelled to Siam in the early part of the eighteenth century. There he settled in Setul where he either began teaching at the town's mosque, which had been established prior to his arrival, or that he himself established the mosque in Setul and began teaching. We are informed that his son, Muhammad, later became the congregational prayer leader (*imām*) in the mosque in Setul. However, we are of the opinion that Muhammad was not simply the congregational prayer leader. Much like his father, he was also the spiritual leader of his congregation. Muhammad's son, Alang Kecil,[3] continued the legacy left to

---

[3] We are confident that this was not his real name. We suspect that this is simply a nickname. The reason being that his father's name and those of his children were proper Muslim names. Added to this, we are proposing that his family may be descended from the Arab world, and therefore, would not have been given a name

him by his forefathers. We are also informed that his daughter, Hamidah, was wed to a man named Saleh. In our opinion, Saleh was one of Alang Kecil's students and a member of his congregation. Since we are not informed of the fate of Alang Kecil's son, Muhammad Saman, it is therefore probable, that Saleh carried on the legacy of his master, the patriarch Alang Kecil, and continued the tradition of scholarship left to him by the latter. Now we are told that Saleh and Hamidah had three children. The eldest, Khatijah, married a man named Ibrahim bin Tahir, popularly known as 'Pak Him', who we believe to have been a student of Saleh and a member of his congregation. We propose that Saleh was very fond of Ibrahim and intended to groom the latter to succeed him as leader of the congregation. Probably, Saleh advised Ibrahim to advance his intellectual scholarship and travel to the holy city of Makkah, giving him references in order to facilitate that end. It is our belief that he did indeed do just that. We know that in the middle of the nineteenth century Ibrahim, along with his bride Khatijah, were in Makkah where Ibrahim was retained as a Quranic teacher at Masjid al-Ḥaram, presumably after the completion of his studies. This would certainly explain how his son, Abdullah, later referred to as Abdullah Fāhim, came to be born there. Ibrahim passed away in Kepala Batas in 1939 and left the continuity of the intellectual tradition familiar to him to his son Abdullah.

---

which did not reflect that heritage. Unfortunately, we are not informed of his real name.

But what of the male ancestry of Abdullah? Earlier we made mention of the fact that factual information about the ancestral lineage of Abdullah Haji Ahmad Badawi is extremely scarce. In fact, the factual information we are referring to is largely vacuous. What we do know is that Abdullah Fāhim was descended from Ibrahim, whose father was Mohammad Tahir, who was descended from Kamaluddin. Now we may assume that Ibrahim's father Mohammad Tahir was the contemporary of Muhammad Saman, whom we referred to earlier. We may further assume that the patriarch Kamaluddin was the contemporary of Alang Kecil. Now one may reasonably pose the question, what, if any, is the connection between Mohammad Tahir and Muhammad Saman, or, for that matter, between Kamaluddin and Alang Kecil? Again we will answer that it is very possible that both Mohammad Tahir and Kamaluddin were members of the religious congregation originally established by Abdul Kadir, either in the capacity of a student or in the capacity of a religious teacher.

Abdullah Fāhim was born in 1869 in Makkah. At the time of his birth, Saudi Arabia as we know it today did not exist. The country was divided into two regions, the Hijāz and the Najd. The former encompassed the entire length of the West coast bordering the Red Sea, while the latter comprised all the lands to the East as far as the Persian Gulf. The Hijāz was governed by the descendants of the Prophet Muhammad; they were the guardians of the two holy cities of Makkah and Madīnah. At the time of Abdullah Fāhim's birth, the Hijāz was governed by al-Amīr al-Sharīf 'Awn al-

Rafīq ibn Muḥammad ibn 'Awn.[4] The family home in Makkah was situated in an area known as Zujāj al-Ḥajar Shu'ayb 'Alī.[5] As a young man in Makkah, Abdullah studied the Islamic sciences including astronomy and the *ḥadīth*. He had a fondness for astronomy as evidenced by the fact that he even had his own observatory complete with an astrolabe, one of his most prized possessions. Among his teachers were 'Umar Bājunayd, 'Abd al-Karīm al-Dāgistānī, Muhammad Mukhtār al-Jāwī, Shaykh As'ad, 'Abd al-Rahmān al-Dahhān and al-Sayyid Muḥammad Amīn ibn al-Sayyid Ahmad ibn 'Allāmah al-Sayyid Riḍwān.[6] It was al-Sayyid Muhammad Amīn Riḍwān who granted Abdullah Fāhim with an *ijāzah*.[7] In the *ijāzah*, the students full name was recorded together with his descent (*nasab*) as being Al-Ḥāj 'Abd Allāh ibn al-Shaykh Ibrāhīm al-Filfilānī al-Jāwī. Like his father before him, Abdullah Fāhim remained in Makkah at the Masjid al-Ḥaram until 1916 teaching the

---

[4] See Mokhtar Petah, *Sheikh Abdullah Fahim: Penentu Tarikh Kemerdekaan Negara 31 Ogos '57* (Kuala Lumpur: Pustaka Antara Sdn. Bhd., 1997), 48.

[5] The land their house was situated on was later taken over by the Government of Saudi Arabia in order to carry out the expansion of Masjid al-Ḥaram.

[6] The names of Abdullah Fāhim's teachers were recorded in his *ijāzah*, granted to him at the completion of his studies. We were not privy to the original manuscript but were able to obtain a printed copy which was given to us by Dr. Badri Najib Zubir, Assistant Professor, Dept. of Arabic Language and Literature, International Islamic University Malaysia.

[7] The *ijāzah* was issued on the 12th of September 1904 (2nd Rajab 1322).

Islamic sciences and the *ḥadīth* to students from all over the world.

We said earlier that it is usual practice for the Arabs to recite their full names which indicate their family name and ancestral origin. Here now in the case of Abdullah Fāhim, we have recorded testimony of his ancestral lineage. The denotation al-Ḥāj indicates that he had performed the pilgrimage. This is followed by his name and the name of his father. The denotation al-Shaykh before his father's name indicates that Abdullah Fāhim's father, Ibrahim, was a scholar. The denotation al-Filfilānī indicates his place of origin. It is important to note that we are sure of the pronunciation of the denotation. It may not be read 'al-Fulfulānī', or even 'al-Falfalānī'. In any case, none holds any meaning in the Arabic language, and we may safely conclude that the term is foreign to the Arabic language. Hence, it is indicative of a region outside the domain of the Arab world. We believe this place to point to a region encompassing what used to be referred to as southern Siam. Since the pronunciation of the denotation should read 'al-Filfilānī', we are confident that the denotation refers to Pulau Pinang. Finally, his descent is indicated by the term al-Jāwī. This means that he was one who spoke a language identified by the Jawi script, in other words, he was a Malay because the Jawi script is particular to the Malays and no one else.[8]

---

[8] See Syed Muhammad Naquib al-Attas, *Islam dalam Sejarah dan Kebudayaan Melayu* (Kuala Lumpur: Angkatan Belia Islam Malaysia (ABIM), 1984).

We mentioned earlier, that Abdullah Fāhim returned to Malaya in 1916. Upon his return, he began teaching at his ancestral home in Kepala Batas before being employed as a teacher for a short while at the Kampung Limbung Kapal Religious School in Alor Setar, Kedah. Much later, after Abdullah Fāhim had left the school, it was renovated and has since been renamed Maktab Mahmud. In reality, Abdullah Fāhim's intentions were to continue the legacy of scholarship and learning originally established by his fore-fathers. To that end, he wished to establish a school of his own, but that would have to wait. Consequently, he made use of the *al-Jāmi' al-Badawī* Mosque in Kepala Batas as his classroom since the *Dā'irat al-Ma'ārif al-Waṭaniyyah*, a religious school which he later founded, had not been conceived yet. Today the school stands next to the mosque across from Abdullah Haji Ahmad Badawi's family home in Kepala Batas. The school is still active and is one of the best *Sekolah Agama Rakyat* in Penang.

In the meantime, the Sultan of Perak offered Abdullah Fāhim the principal's post at the Idrīsiyyah Religious School in Kuala Kangsar, Perak. Since we have established the fact that the *Dā'irat al-Ma'ārif al-Wataniyyah* had not been conceived, he accepted the job. So in 1931, his wife and young son, Ahmad Badawi, went with him to live in Kuala Kangsar. Towards the end of his tenure however, Abdullah Fāhim fell victim to slander and envy and was henceforth relieved of his duties at the school. He returned to Kepala Batas in January of 1945 with a heavy heart, but would continue to guide the curriculum of the school for eighteen years.

It is said, that several weeks after his removal, an envoy from Kuala Kangsar was dispatched to Kepala Batas to meet with him. Apparently, since Abdullah Fāhim's departure, the water wells in Kuala Kangsar had dried up and rumour began to spread that the cause was a result of the unjust treatment Abdullah Fāhim had received while in Kuala Kangsar. It was commonly held that Abdullah Fāhim was a saintly man, so the mysterious water shortage was held to be the result of his anger towards the unjustified slander leveled against him. The envoy duly begged for forgiveness which was granted, and was told to return to Kuala Kangsar. "All would be well," assured Abdullah Fāhim, and indeed upon the envoy's return to Kuala Kangsar, he found the wells to be brimming with water.[9]

When his disciples and the people who knew him are asked about their opinion of Abdullah Fāhim, their recollections are all anecdotal in nature. Below are some of the more commonly related anecdotes concerning his character. A word of caution however, we are not including these anecdotes simply for the purpose of trying to glorify this particular aspect of our subject. It is simply due to the fact that in constructing a plausible biography of his life and character, apart from describing his intellectual capacity, we wish to show the humanitarian side of Abdullah Fāhim.

Once, while in Butterworth, Abdullah Fāhim hailed a taxi to take him home to Kepala Batas. Normally, the taxi

---

[9] This story was narrated to us by Dato' Mohd. Noor Ahmad, in Kepala Batas during our visit to his home on the 15th August of 2004.

driver would hope for at least four people to occupy his car before embarking on the journey which would normally cost two dollars, an average of 50 cents per person. On this day however, Abdullah Fāhim was his only fare. On the way to Kepala Batas, the taxi driver began to daydream. "How nice it would be if I could earn five dollars from this fare", thought the taxi driver. He started thinking of all the things he would be able to do with the money. This occupied his mind until they arrived in Kepala Batas. Abdullah Fāhim disembarked, dug deep into his pockets and handed the taxi driver five dollars. The taxi driver was amazed and hastily tried to return the change. Abdullah Fāhim then said, "This is what you wanted is it not?"[10]

Such was the character of Abdullah Fāhim. No one ever dreamed of accepting money as payment from him. Whenever he had coffee at one of the local coffee shops, the proprietor felt it was an honour and would subsequently refuse to accept any compensation. As a result, Abdullah Fāhim had to devise an ingenious method of payment; he would slip the money underneath the cup before he left. That cup would then be fought over by subsequent patrons to the coffee shop.[11]

Everyone who knew him, or who knew of him, considered him to be one possessed of saintly qualities through whom God works (karāmāt). It is worth mentioning here, that these saintly qualities are not simply manifested by the aforementioned portrayals of wisdom and knowledge

---

[10] Ibid.
[11] Ibid.

characterised by an extra sensory perception. There are several ranks (*marātib*) of saintly qualities, the lowest of which is manifest as the aforementioned portrayals. The more noble rank is characterised by the legacy of Islamic scholarship and learning established during one's lifetime, and punctuated by the establishment of a tradition which continues even after one has died. Then there is the rank bestowed by God and reserved for His Prophets[12] which represents the most noble rank. Consequently, the Prophets possess all the ranks, but the converse is not true. In other words, one possessed of saintly qualities from the lowest rank cannot also be said to be possessed of qualities from the more nobler ranks.

As far as Abdullah Fāhim is concerned, it is our opinion that he was possessed of the second aforementioned rank. The establishment of the *Dā'irat al-Ma'ārif al-Waṭaniyyah* and its continuing tradition of Islamic learning and scholarship bears testament to this fact. The school was established in 1935. At the time of its establishment, it was referred to as being a *sekolah pondok*, so named because the students who flocked to the school erected huts around the school compounds where they would stay, much like a boarding school. However, unlike other schools classified using the same designation, the *Dā'irat al-Ma'ārif al-Waṭaniyyah*

---

[12] This gift allows Prophets to perform miracles (*mu'jizāt*) that God works through them, like for instance having the capacity to raise the dead, as was the case with the Prophet 'Īsā (a.s.), or to be able to part the Red sea, as was the case with the Prophet Mūsā (a.s.), or by the miracle of the Qur'ān, as is the case with the Prophet Muḥammad (s.a.w.).

conducted classes according to the more traditional Islamic education system in tandem with the modern curriculum employed by the public school system. For example, lectures would be conducted after normal school hours. These lectures, referred to as general studies, would be open to the public regardless of their status or intellectual capacity.[13] Much of his intellectual discourses and mystical poetic compositions are now housed in the diminutive library of the school. In addition, apart from the numerous reference manuals and works authored by Abdullah Fāhim, it is a little known fact that he devised a prayer almanac (*taqwīm*), possibly the first of its kind in this country. The almanac would become an indispensable tool in correctly and accurately determining the times for prayer. His knowledge of astronomy and the familiarity with which he deftly handled his astrolabe would later make it possible for him to predict, using a six figure algorithm, the most suitable date for Malaya to declare independence.

In politics subsequent to Malaya's Independence in 1957, Abdullah Fāhim became Penang's first official expounder of Islamic law (*mufti*), and held the post until 1961. Prior to that, when UMNO was first established in 1946, Abdullah Fāhim was introduced to UMNO's founder and first President, Dato' Onn Ja'afar. The former was so impressed by Dato' Onn's intelligence, charismatic appeal and purposeful determination to unite the Malays, that he

---

[13] This fact was relayed to us by Dato' Haji Arshad Haji Zakaria, Congregation Chairman of the Masjid al-Jāmi 'al-Badawī during our visit to Kepala Batas on the 15th of August 2004.

offered himself as the first UMNO member of Seberang Perai. In fact, it was Dato' Onn himself who pinned the badge of UMNO on the lapel of Abdullah Fāhim's shirt. The latter proudly wore his badge like a symbol of courage and virtue, never removing it even until the day he died. Abdullah Fāhim was actively involved in the country's struggle for independence. He played a pivotal role in providing spiritual guidance. He is known in Malaysian history as the man who determined the date of Independence to be the 31st of August 1957.[14] The truth of this fact was relayed directly to the current Prime Minister by Tunku Abdul Rahman himself. "As a scholar, he had many followers among whom were directly involved in the struggle for independence. His words of advice to them were to be sincere in their struggle, to avoid abusing the positions and power they were entrusted with and to alienate themselves from greed and corruption".[15]

Apparently, Sardon Jubir, who was the UMNO Youth leader at the time, introduced Abdullah Fāhim to Tunku Abdul Rahman Putra al-Haj, when Tunku was seeking a suitable date for Malaya to seek independence. It is said that Sardon Jubir along with Abdullah's father, Ahmad Badawi, who was the deputy UMNO Youth leader at the time, held consultations with Abdullah Fāhim regarding a suitable date for Malaya's independence. Abdullah Fāhim advised that

---

[14] See Mokhtar Petah, *Sheikh Abdullah Fahim Penentu Tarikh Kemerdekaan Negara 31 Ogos '57* (Kuala Lumpur: Pustaka Antara Sdn. Bhd., 1997).

[15] NSTP Research & Information Service, "Spiritual Leader and UMNO Pioneer", *Sunday Mail*, 16th November 2003.

the date chosen had to be calculated, based on his own celestial calculations. It was calculated, after long drawn discussions and much serious thought, that the 31st of August 1957 would be the most suitable and auspicious date to declare independence.[16] In fact, according to some sources,[17] when Tunku Abdul Rahman was advised of the date, he was also advised to travel by ship to England via Karachi. The reason was to allow time for the Merdeka Mission delegates to thoroughly refine their strategy. It would defeat the purpose to travel in haste only to be disappointed by the outcome. When all had agreed to formally ask for independence, and if it was granted, then Tunku should hasten back to Malaya by air. This is exactly what took place. The Merdeka Mission delegates travelled to Karachi by ship, all the while discussing their strategy. Having obtained a unanimous consensus with regard to demanding independence from the British, the delegates hastened to England by air so as not to afford any of the delegates a change of heart. After getting the agreement of the British, Tunku Abdul Rahman and the other Merdeka Mission delegates hastened back to Malaya to deliver the good news.[18]

In the aforementioned meeting, it was reported that Abdullah F him predicted that Tunku Abdul Rahman would

---

[16] Cecilia Tan, *Tun Sardon Jubir: His Life & Times* (Petaling Jaya: Pelanduk Publications, 1986).

[17] This story was narrated to us by Dato' Mohd. Noor Ahmad in Kepala Batas during our visit to his home on the 15th of August 2004.

[18] See Mohamed Abid, *Reflections of Pre-Independence Malaya* (Petaling Jaya: Pelanduk Publications, 2004), 2nd ed.

only govern Malaya for seven years at most before Malaya would adopt a new name. Upon hearing this, Tunku Abdul Rahman remarked, "What will happen after that?" Abdullah Fāhim calmly replied, "What happens after that is up to you; it is for you to decide what to call this country." As it happens, Tunku Abdul Rahman governed Malaya for precisely six years and sixteen days. Henceforth, Malaya would be called Malaysia.[19]

Three months before his death on the 28th of April 1961, Abdullah Fāhim was strolling past one of the coffee shops in Kepala Batas. It so happens, that one of his earliest students, a man by the name of Ahmad Hashimi, was sitting at the coffee shop reading the *Utusan Melayu* newspaper which had printed a story about Abdullah Haji Ahmad Badawi's appointment as the representative of *Gabungan Pelajar-Pelajar Melayu Semenanjung*,[20] or GPMS to its Annual General Assembly. Abdullah Fāhim asked Ahmad Hashimi what he was reading. The latter replied, "I am reading about Abdullah". "Which Abdullah?", was the formers reply. "Your grandson Abdullah", replied Ahmad and duly showed him the column. Abdullah Fāhim quietly read the piece, and after about a minute or so remarked, "At some point in the future, Abdullah will become the leader of the government".[21] Abdullah Haji Ahmad

---

[19] Related to us by Dato' Haji Mohd. Noor Ahmad during our visit to Kepala Batas on the 15th of August 2004.

[20] Loosely translated as *The Malay Students Association of the Peninsula*.

[21] This story was narrated to us by Dato' Mohd. Noor Ahmad in Kepala Batas during our visit to his home on the 15th of August 2004.

Badawi's appointment as Prime Minister fulfils the words of his grandfather. Abdullah Fāhim died at the age of 92 and is buried in the compound of the *al-Jāmi' al-Badawī* Mosque in Kepala Batas.

THREE

THE PREDICAMENT

IN THE PROLOGUE, we have made mention of the fact that in order to sufficiently and adequately explain what is truly meant by the phrase 'Islam hadhari' requires an intellectual understanding of the present situation. But why would one concern oneself with this notion which is apparently politically motivated? After all, did we not mention the fact that it is not in one's nature to be overly preoccupied with matters concerning politics? If that were true, why then does one feel the need to detach oneself from intellectual pursuit and transcend into matters of politics? To begin with, we believe that this is a nation looking for a new foundation, and that the Prime Minister is looking for people with the ability to speak their minds and to articulate ideas. He has even said himself, "that the time for action is overdue".[1] In light of

---

[1] See the article "Muslim world needs a meeting of minds" published in the *New Straits Times*, Tuesday, the 5th of October 2004.

this, we may answer that we would not have concerned ourselves were it not for the feeble attempts to explain what is
meant by the Prime Minister by those claiming to
understand, yet who are instead trying to legitimise such a
phrase by emphasising Islām, as though Islām itself had
become a handmaiden to the political arena. In addition, if it
were simply a political manoeuvre to swing the electorate in
favour of UMNO, it would not be cause for concern. More
importantly however, recent attempts by those same people
to indoctrinate this phrase into the curriculum of both local
universities and institutions of higher learning without, we
believe, first having a firm grasp of what is meant, has
effectively made it incumbent upon the scholar to first
comprehend what is being sought in order that he may
adequately explain it for the benefit of those entrusted with
administering and effectuating a shift towards this idea.

Also in the prologue, we have made mention of the fact
that the idea for 'Islam hadhari' is generally ascribed to the
prominent leader, statesman, master administrator and political luminary, Abdullah Haji Ahmad Badawi, the fifth Prime
Minister of Malaysia. We use the term 'ascribed' because in
reality, the current Prime Minister inherited this approach
from the administration of his predecessor. The idea was
originally meant only as a tool to swing the Malay electoral
vote in favour of the most prominent influential and power-
ful Malay political organisation today, the United Malays
National Organisation (UMNO). The Muslim opposition, in
trying to garner electoral favour from the Malays, had
portrayed its political agenda as being the sole recipient of
endorsement by Islām, only its members could be consider-

ed the true guardians of Islām, and only its political organisation could be determined to be the one remaining repository
of Islām. The political platform of the Muslim opposition in
recent years appeared to suggest that only those professing
allegiance to its organisation could copiously partake of
libations from the vessel that appeared to emphasise Islām at
its core. The Prime Minister himself mentions that:

> "the pan-Malaysia Islamic party has politicised
> religion to the extent that it claims a monopoly on
> Islām. They canvass for votes by telling villagers that
> they would be assured of heaven if they vote for their
> party. They have been known to decree members and
> supporters of my party as infidels".[2]

Sadly, the Muslim opposition's preoccupation with the
ritualistic aspect of Islām coupled with a fervent inadequate
elementary understanding of the legal aspects of Islām, and
of Islām in general, sowed the seeds of transformation, thus
allowing an original ideal to descend into the realm of that
approaching tyranny. In order to combat this apparent down-
ward spiral, which is clearly effecting the Muslim majority
and society at large, the introduction of a more reasonable
and balanced approach to the problems facing the Muslims
was proposed by the former administration. Consequently,
the task of conceptualising an adequate response was
entrusted to the universities and institutions of higher
learning. What these universities and institutions of higher
learning proposed was the idea of a progressive, 'civilisa-

---

[2] Ibid.

tional' Islām, or 'Islam hadhari'. At the time of its proposal, the idea was understood as a way of undermining the Muslim opposition, which was viewed as being lost in a maze of confusion, only concerned with demolishing proposals put forth by their detractors. In addition, it was primarily concerned with trying to introduce an idea or way of thinking geared towards improving the economic opportunities of the Malays. In contrast, the Muslim opposition did not have an answer for those seeking economic progress and development, and failed to recognise the predicament of the Muslims, both in this country and in the rest of the Muslim world.

But what is the present predicament of the Muslims in this country? When we refer to the Muslims in this context, we are invariably referring to the Malays. When we speak of the Malays in this context, we are also invariably referring to their political history, which means we must consider the role of 'the struggle of UMNO'. In order to adequately do so, the onus of responsibility must be duly apportioned. This in itself poses another problem. Whenever one has made inquiry into the question of responsibility with reference to the 'struggle of UMNO', the answer has always been one of caution, or the inquiry itself has been met with allegations of sensitivity. This response begs the question, sensitive to what? It cannot be sensitive to the truth because that would be antithetical not only to the National Constitution, but to the very Constitution of UMNO whose very purpose was prefaced on the Malays themselves. The next logical question then, would be to ask, sensitive to whom? It cannot be sensitive to the Malays because it is in their own interest to understand their history. The former Prime Minister himself "believed in learning the lessons of history".[3] Neither can it be sensitive to the other races because it is in their own interest to have a stable form of government. Hence, one may only conclude that this sensitivity implies one or several individuals. If this were true, then the next logical question would be to ask, how do the interests of one or a handful of individuals concerned with their own agenda determine the path of an entire nation?

UMNO was established as a political organisation in 1946 by its founder and first President, Dato' Onn Ja'afar. At the time, its motives were clear. Its purpose was to force the British colonial government to surrender political control of the country to the Malays who had suffered great injustice at the hands of the colonialists. Dato' Onn's role was to unite the Malays and gather them into a force to be reckoned with. It was this element of unity that finally managed to wrest power from the British colonial government. So how was this unity achieved? Was it achieved through persuasion? Was it achieved by appealing to moral responsibility? Was it attained as a result of political manoeuvring and a challenge which confronted the emotional fighting spirit of the Malays? Indeed unity was achieved through all the aforementioned methods. However, the one primary essential element which guaranteed unity amongst the Malays, was in defining who the Malays were. The contemporary

---

[3] See the foreword of the Prime Minister contained in Mohamed Abid's *Reflections of Pre-Independence Malaya* (Petaling Jaya: Pelanduk Publications, 2004), 2nd ed.

definition of 'Malay' tends to concentrate more on a phenotypic description of the Malays which portrays a more anthropological view. Far from being a unifying element, this type of description results in the classification of the Malays into different segregated groups because each group would be identified by certain characteristics peculiar to each phenotype. So what is the unifying element that correctly defines the Malays?

Dato' Onn defined the term 'Malay' in a concise, philosophico-scientific historical manner. According to him, a Malay is defined as being one who is a Muslim, this is paramount because it is this element which gives one identity. The identity of the Malay is further defined as being one who speaks the Malay language, whose roots are firmly based on the Arabic language, followed by one whose customs and traditions are said to be Malay. Again, these customs and traditions are derived from the fundamental elements of the worldview of Islām.[4] Dato' Onn clearly understood that the cloak of Islām was the unifying element for all Muslims. Since the language and cultural traditions of

---

[4] Some may argue that the customs and traditions of the Malays are derived in large part from Hinduism. We do not argue that some cultural traditions were borrowed from Hinduism, but we have emphasised the fact that Malay customs and traditions are derived from the fundamental elements of the worldview of Islām. This means that once Islām was adopted, cultural practices and traditions which were alien to Islām underwent a process known as *islamisation*. For a further elucidation of the term 'islamisation' and its related elements, see Syed Muhammad Naquib al-Attas, *Islam and Secularism* (Kuala Lumpur: International Institute of Islamic Thought and Civilization (ISTAC), 1993).

the Malays are derived from Islām,[5] the religion itself had to be the unifying element. One may conclude therefore, that UMNO was founded upon an Islamic platform because it was this definition that at once unified every traditional group regardless of their ancestry. For further confirmation of the fact that the unifying element for the Malays was Islām, a perusal of Dato' Onn's rousing political speeches would not be in vain. For example, if one were to examine the contents of his speech delivered at the first Malay Congress held at the Sultan Sulaiman Club in Kuala Lumpur in March of 1946, Dato' Onn clearly states that, "Today we aim to create the foundations for that which we have longed for, [which is to create] unity amongst us".[6] Note that he does not say, "Today we aim to create the foundations for that which we have longed for, [which is to create] an independent nation", or "We aim to create the foundations for that which we have longed for, [which is to] seek independence". The emphasis is on unity. As we have said earlier, that unity may only be achieved by first defining the Malays according to their religious allegiance, because without Islām, there could be no Malay language or civilisation. He goes on to say, "The unity of our nation may only be preserved by holding fast to an ideal, which is grander and nobler than us all". The ideal referred to here can only be interpreted as being the religion of Islām, which is the very identity of the Malay race. Further on, Dato' Onn mentions

---

[5] Ibid., 169-183. See also Syed Muhammad Naquib al-Attas, *Islam dalam Sejarah dan Kebudayaan Melayu* (Kuala Lumpur: Angkatan Belia Islam Malaysia (ABIM), 1984).

[6] *Reflections of Pre-Independence Malaya*, 184.

that, "We want to see the unity amongst us realised. [We want to see, that this] is given all the support and assistance [needed] *according to the demands of our time*".[7] The latter part of the previous sentence will be of importance later on when discussing the meaning of 'Islam hadhari'. We do not need to linger on the fact that it was Islām that was the unifying element for the Malays. The current Prime Minister himself acknowledges that, "The Malays, UMNO and Islām in this country cannot be separated. Together, the elements form a distinct culture and identity".[8] However, one needs to emphasise that this very salient fact regarding the political history of the Malays appears to have either been largely ignored, or has failed to grasp the comprehension of the historian.

So what was it that caused the unity of the Malays to once again revert to discord and disunity? The Muslim opposition claims to have established an organisation founded on an Islamic platform, and yet the consequence cannot be said to be that of a united Muslim front. Can the failure be attributed to Islām? Or can the failure be attributed to an ignorance of Islām? The religion of Islām itself is perfect, as indicated by the verse in the Qur'ān:

---

[7] See *Reflections of Pre-Independence Malaya*, 184. The use of italics is my own only to show emphasis.
[8] See the Prime Minister's keynote address delivered at the UMNO General Assembly on the 23rd of September 2004 in Kuala Lumpur.

56

This day I have perfected your religion for you, completed My favour upon you, and have chosen for you Islām as your religion.[9]

Hence, the latter must be the case. Therefore, instead of Islām becoming the unifying element, it has perhaps become a mere slogan in the political arena, wielded at will to lend authority to any political agenda seeking endorsement. Unlike the Muslim opposition, the Constitution of UMNO, and indeed of Malaysia, cannot endorse this caricature to religion.

We have mentioned earlier that Dato' Onn's definition was founded upon his acute, concise, philosophico-scientific historical knowledge of the Malays. What resulted was unity punctuated by the establishment of the United Malays National Organisation. If this unity is no longer apparent today, and if the Malays today "may be classified as being like a mother still suffering from labour pains",[10] it is only natural that UMNO struggle to once again seek to establish itself as the unifying element for the Malays. In UMNO's attempts to do so, it has introduced the now-in-vogue phrase 'Islam hadhari', which representatives of the government claim was being practised since Independence with Tunku Abdul Rahman Putra Al-Haj at the helm,[11] and has entrusted

---

[9] 5/al-Mā'idah, 3. Translation of the verse is from Abdullah Yusuf Ali, *The Meaning of the Holy Qur'ān* (Brentwood, Maryland: Amana Corporation, 1991).

[10] See Dato' Onn's letter to *Utusan Melayu* found in *Reflections of Pre-Independence Malaya*, op. cit., 178.

[11] See the *New Straits Times*, Monday, the 27th of September 2004, 14. In an article entitled "RTM to screen series on Islam Hadhari",

the dissemination of its inherent meaning to the local universities and institutions of higher learning, which were apparently established on the basis of a firm grasp and an understanding of 'Islam hadhari'.[12] If indeed this was the case, why does an apparent difficulty in defining the phrase persist? If 'Islam hadhari' is understood to indicate a progressive approach to development, why does this idea begin with Tunku Abdul Rahman? No doubt his administration emphasised progressive development, but what about the approach pursued by Dato' Onn Ja'afar?

One has only to peruse the political speeches of Dato' Onn Ja'afar to realise that what his administration intended was not merely directed towards seeking independence from the British colonial government, nor was it intended solely for the establishment of Malay political power, or towards advancing the economic lot of the Malays. The bigger intention had to do with seeking to struggle against the unenviable bestial character of man, in this case the Malays, that was at times, incapable of accepting criticism, that was prone to slander (*fitnah*), envy (*ḥasad*), jealousy, arrogance (*takabbur*), greed and a subservience towards an unjust

---

the Deputy Minister of Information, Datuk Zainuddin Maidin is quoted as saying, "Islam Hadhari is not new. From Tunku Abdul Rahman's era until today, the government has always practised Islam Hadhari".

[12] Ibid. In the same article, the Deputy Minister of Information is also quoted as saying, "This (i.e. the practice of Islam Hadhari since the time of Tunku Abdul Rahman) is also evident in the setting up of Bank Islam, Tabung Haji, International Islamic University and other establishments for the benefit of the Muslims, based on Islamic requirements".

authority. For example, Dato' Onn mentioned that, "There were two places the Malays wanted to exhibit themselves haughtily: One, was to their neighbours; the other, was to the enemy of the Malays ... one should not consider striving for position alone, while rejecting one's own race".[13] One may reasonably infer that what Dato' Onn meant was that there are at least two kinds of Malay; one that is prone to succumb to the aforementioned characteristics, and one that is not. With reference to the one that is prone to the previously mentioned vile characteristics, Dato' Onn says, "I previously referred to the matter of danger that surrounds the Malays of this Peninsula, without needing to mention from which other party [this danger originates. I will say, that this danger] originates from the Malays themselves".[14] Does this danger Dato' Onn refers to point to a danger which is external to Malays? Or does this danger referred to by him point to ignorance as a consequence of allowing the bestial nature of the Malays to become manifest? Let us preface by saying that the latter is true. In order to understand what is

---

[13] See *Reflections of Pre-Independence Malaya*. The Malay text reads, "ada dua tempat orang Melayu hendak bertenggek; satu kepada jiran, satu kepada musuh Melayu". See *Peristiwa-Peristiwa Sebelum Kemerdekaan Malaya*, 214. The term 'bertenggek' in the Malay language literally means 'to perch', much like a bird on a branch. In this context however, the term 'to perch' does not convey intelligible meaning. And therefore, one has to make a scholarly interpretation of what is meant. When a bird is perched on a branch, for instance, it preens its feathers at times to attract attention to itself, or perhaps to make itself attractive to the opposite sex. It is this act of preening to draw attention to itself which is a haughty exhibition.

[14] Ibid., 250.

meant by Dato' Onn in reference to the Malays being the greatest danger to themselves, one must first understand the nature of man.[15]

Man is a single individual being having a dual nature. On the creation of man, the Qur'ān mentions he has a body which belongs to the animal species and a spirit foreign to that species; it is that spirit that governs the body either for good or for bad. Man has been given knowledge about the nature of things, for God taught man the names[16] of everything in order to know their relations and understand their meanings in the order of existence. According to the Holy Qur'ān, man is given some knowledge about his spirit.[17] Indeed this knowledge is very profound for man and cannot be exhausted, but however little, is sufficient for man to understand his nature, and will ultimately lead to knowledge about the nature of God. The Qur'ān speaks of the spirit as a single entity, an individual which is referred to as the heart (*al-qalb*), the soul (*al-nafs*), the intellect (*al-'aql*) and the spirit (*al-rūh*). These four terms are different activities all pointing to a single entity, the spirit. It is known by many names because it is always in activity manifesting

---

[15] For the following discussion on the nature of man, we have summarised the ideas of Syed Muhammad Naquib al-Attas contained in chapter four of the *Prolegomena to the Metaphysics of Islām. An Exposition of the Fundamental Elements of the Worldview of Islām* (Kuala Lumpur: International Institute of Islamic Thought and Civilization (ISTAC), 1995), 143-176. Henceforth cited as *Prolegomena*.

[16] Not necessarily the essences or nature of that spirit itself, rather the attributes of things.

[17] Meaning his self.

itself in one of the aforementioned moulds. Because man has been given knowledge about the nature of God, he is bound by a covenant where he has recognised God, is conscious of who He is, has affirmed the truth and has acknowledged God as his Lord, as a result of which man knows who he is and what he must do. Knowledge of the self is also bound by this covenant, for the understanding of man's self[18] will lead to the understanding of his Lord.

Man is bound by the religion of Islām,[19] consciously and willingly in submission. In spite of man's forgetful nature, he has been given intellect, he has certain faculties of the

---

[18] What is meant, is that his true self is the one that had made the covenant with God. Some deviationist interpretations have mistakenly interpreted Lord to mean the self. Syed Muhammad Naquib al-Attas has argued knowing the Lord to be if one returns to the state one was before, one will know the Lord, as the souls on the day of the covenant knew the Lord.

[19] The Qur'ān refers to two kinds of submission; willingly and grudgingly. The latter is not what is meant by Islām. Islām, in this sense in willing and conscious submission of the entire self during the whole of ones ethical life. In Islām, everything has to be done with conscious intention. Man is also forgetful, for after having made the covenant with God, he forgot to fulfil that covenant. Following the interpretation of *insān* according to Ibn 'Abbās, the word *insān*, to a certain extent, tells us about the nature of man, that he is forgetful. In the chapter entitled "Islām: The Concept of Religion and the Foundation of Ethics and Morality" which comprises Chapter One of the *Prolegomena*, the authour elucidates on the forgetfulness of man giving the example, when man was born he did not know anything, and now as an adult he has forgotten what he was like before. Therefore forgetfulness is man's nature, in spite of which the Qur'ān exhorts us to remember (*dhikir*) and consequently the purpose of religion is to return man to that state of awareness.

senses and interestingly enough, hearing is the last of the senses to develop because it is through this sense that knowledge in general is received.[20] Man has been equipped with intelligence to guide himself, to be able to distinguish between truth and fabrication, and between right and wrong. In order to clarify what is meant, let us refer to the story of the Prophet Ibrāhīm. When the Prophet contemplated the stars and thought that they were God, he discovered the stars would set so he fixed his attention on the moon, reasoning its size and illuminative power to be God until he discovered that like the stars, it also set. Finally, his assumptions led him to presume the sun to be God, until he discovered that the sun also set. Ultimately he asked God to guide him, to show him the truth. This example lends to the activity of the intellect and reason and exhibits the limitations of reason when making conclusions about the knowledge of God.

The epistemological implications of the four terms describing the spirit as a single entity can be derived from a linguistic understanding of these terms. For example, *al-nafs* implies breath, from the root *nafasa* which indicates a condition of activity. Hence, the reality of man is something which is not static, rather is it dynamic and always in a state of activity. After all it originates, in a certain sense, from the breath of God Himself, and God is a being that is not static but dynamic without any change or transformation occurring

---

[20] Sages of the past have listed hearing as the last of the senses to develop, to hear the truth, to hear the words of truth because the revelation is transmitted through that sense. When they speak of the *mushāhadah*, they talk about inclining one's ear in contemplation as if to listen intently.

in Him, without becoming, He is always as He was. He is not in the sense of what Aristotle described Him to be: Unmoved and immutable.[21]

These terms have a dual meaning; on the one hand, they refer to something material; on the other hand, to something non-material. With reference to the material meaning of the word 'heart', it refers to the organ contained in the left side of the breast that circulates blood[22] to the rest of the body. With regard to the material meaning of the term 'soul', it is the individual being before us. Similarly the intellect, the material aspect of which is the manifestation of the activities of the brain; although the brain is only an instrument of the intellect but somehow the activity of the soul is located, or concentrated in function, in the brain. These four terms indicate indivisible, identical identities that are not measured in terms of time and space; it is something created. The only way to know it is to know the observable activities that issue from it, or its nature as such, cannot be understood.

As far as the non-material meaning of these terms, the Muslims understand 'heart' to be a spiritual organ of cognition that receives intuitive illumination; the 'intellect', also a spiritual organ that intellects, that is active, that is constantly contemplating the realities of things; the 'self' refers to that

---

[21] This points to the Islamic conception of God being different from that of the Western conception of God in ancient times.

[22] Early Muslim writers refer to blood as the animal life that courses throughout the body, and that it is the vehicle of the animal spirit bringing life to all parts of the body. When blood no longer circulates through the body, the body is then termed 'dead'.

soul that answers, "Yea! We do testify",[23] to God's "Am I not your Lord (Who cherishes and sustains you)?";[24] the 'spirit' is perhaps a collective name for all four when it is in abstraction. With regard to man, there are good and bad qualities pertaining to the body. Therefore, on the animal soul, it is generally understood to mean inclining to what is contradictory to the rational soul.[25] The Qur'ān mentions, in general, there are three states of this soul; the soul that has achieved tranquillity and peace, that is constantly in remembrance of its covenant with God, is referred to as the tranquil soul (*al-nafs al-muṭma'innah*). It is no longer in a

[23] 7/al-A'rāf, 172. Translation of the verse is from Abdullah Yusuf Ali, *The Meaning of the Holy Qur'ān* (Brentwood, Maryland: Amana Corporation, 1991).

[24] Ibid.

[25] The explanation afforded by the author of the *Prolegomena*, is that one should not take this to mean that Islām is denigrating the body, for this would be contrary to the teachings of Islām. The body also has beneficial purpose; it is made in a beautiful form, to preserve oneself when sick and so on. The body itself is useful in the acquisition of knowledge. Man is created in perfection, as a being peculiar to himself, at the same time his animal nature drags him down to the lowest of the low where sometimes what is evil in man is worse than even animals. This is confirmed by the Qur'ān, "They have hearts wherewith they understand not, eyes wherewith they see not, and ears wherewith they hear not. They are like cattle —nay more misguided: for they are heedless (of warning)", (7/al-A'rāf, 179). But the Qur'ān makes an exception: "Except such as have faith (*īmān*), and do righteous deeds", (103/al-'Aṣr, 3). Those people remain in the best of moulds. It is therefore against the conflicting natures of the animal powers that the Prophet Muḥammad referred to upon returning from battle when he said; "Now we are returning from the smaller *jihād* to the greater *jihād*", that is to say the *jihād* against the self (referring to the animal soul).

state of vacillation. Additionally, there is the soul that tries to improve itself, is always criticising itself and looking into all its faults that is referred to as the soul that censures itself (*al-nafs al-lawwāmah*). And finally, the soul that is inclined to evil, or that incites evil (*al-nafs al-ammārah bi'l-sū'*).

Suffice it to say, that if the Malays persist down a path of intellectual catatonia towards their religion, history and philosophy, while at the same time allow the aforementioned vile bestial characteristics to manifest themselves, verily this will be their undoing. This further reminds us of something related to us by Sayyidinā 'Alī ibn Abī Ṭālib (may Allāh be pleased with him). One day, two arrogant men were in the company of 'Alī ibn Abī Ṭālib bragging about themselves. All the while, Sayyidinā 'Alī patiently endured their pompous, vainglorious arrogance. Then he asked them, "Are both of you so proud of the fact that your bodies are decaying, while your souls are in hellfire? If you both had work, then you would have responsibility; and if you both had morals, then you would have honour; and if both of you were devout, then you would have nobility, otherwise the donkey is better than the both of you; and the both of you are no better than anyone".[26]

So have the Malays heeded the admonitions of Dato' Onn? We may answer by saying that indeed, both the former Prime Minister, Tun Dr. Mahathir Mohamad, and the current Prime Minister have understood and have heeded the advice. In Dr. Mahathir's case, throughout the twenty two years of

---

[26] Muhammad Muflih al-Maqdisi, *Al-Adāb Al-Shar'iyyah* (Beirut: Al-Risalah Publishing House, 1997), 201. Translation my own.

his administration, and even before, he continuously encouraged the Malays to rid themselves of the aforementioned vile bestial characteristics plaguing them. Some of his writings critical of the Malay character bear testament to this fact. But are those entrusted by their leaders to shoulder the task of implementing changes in accordance with their admonitions doing so? We cannot say that this is so in reference to the Muslim opposition. But let us not be misled into believing that UMNO is exempt from the burden of responsibility, given the fact that the President of the organisation who is also the Prime Minister, admitted that "we have ourselves to blame".[27] If the collective voice of UMNO fails to recognise their shortcomings, the problems of disunity and ignorance will persist. But should UMNO alone accept the burden of responsibility and accountability?

The Malays now are suffering from a crisis of identity. Earlier, we have made mention of the fact that the task of conceptualising an adequate political response to the encroachment of the political platform espoused by the Muslim opposition, was entrusted to the local universities and institutions of higher learning. It is now clear, judging from reports in the local media and from allegations of responsibility emerging from certain academic institutions,

---

[27] See the article "Muslim world needs a meeting of minds" published in the *New Straits Times*, Tuesday, the 5th of October 2004. Although in the article the Prime Minister is primarily referring to the wretched economic conditions of Muslims throughout the world, he appears to be more concerned with the perception of Islām by the West and with the current ignorance towards Islām by the Muslims themselves.

that this was indeed the case. UMNO rightly sought the 'expert' opinion of its so called 'scholars' to conceptualise a framework which would at once answer the critics with regard to the current plight of the Muslims, which we have said was the result of ignorance and disunity. We use the term 'rightly' because in matters of religion, UMNO does not see itself as an authority. The Prime Minister correctly explains, that:

"The observance of the canon of accountability in Islam was often matched by respect for [the views of men of authority in learning]. Morally upright caliphs accommodated opinions that were different from theirs. In fact, there is a hadith that even eulogises differences of opinion within the ummah as a sign of blessing. It explains why, at different points in Muslim history, there were healthy discussions and debates about religious matters among scholars and segments of the populace".[28]

---

[28] Ibid. Square brackets found in the quotation above are my own addition. The original text reads "The observance of the canon of accountability in Islam was often matched by respect for the people's views". We believe this to be an erroneous statement because in order to accept accountability, one must have prior knowledge of that which one will ultimately be held accountable for. And therefore, this requires that the one accepting accountability, must himself be one who is an authority in that particular field of knowledge required. This fact is confirmed later in the aforementioned quote, by saying that "there were healthy discussions and debates about religious matters among scholars and segments of the populace".

Therefore, in order to correctly assess problems arising from ignorance with regard to religion, it has rightly referred those matters to those they deem to be the authority, in this case, the local universities and institutions of higher learning, principally those claiming to be authorities on Islām. They in turn, are in consultation with the relevant government ministries, *sharī'ah* boards, and the Islamic Council. Together, they devise a solution and their recommendations are forwarded.

We previously posed the question with regard to where the onus of responsibility lies. We may now conclude that the onus of responsibility lies with those charged with the assumption of authority. It is they who claim that history and philosophy have become irrelevant. Their inability to make definitions, and ignorance with regard to knowledge of Islām, history, philosophy and Islamic thought in general, bears testament to this fact. According to them, what is needed now is not history or philosophy, but rather a profound grasp of the holy Qur'ān and the Sunnah[29] of the Prophet (God's prayer and peace be upon him), in tandem with a recondite comprehension of the first obligatory to all Muslims (*fard 'ayn*) and of the other obligatory to some

---

[29] While the Qur'ān is inspired by Allāh in letter as well as in meaning, the *hadīth*'s are the inspired judgments and guidance of the Prophet (God's prayer and peace be upon him) on various matters of Islamic practice. In other words, the *hadīth*'s are in the Prophet's own words and are, in this sense, different from the Qur'ān, though they are to be seen as part and parcel of each other and of the message of Islām. The aggregate effect of the *hadīth*'s—the statements, acts and sanctions of the Prophet is called the Sunnah of the Prophet.

Muslims (*fard kifāyah*).[30] With regard to the first obligatory to all Muslims, this should not pose a problem if the tenets of the religion of Islām are correctly understood. With regard to the other obligatory to some Muslims, the reason it is only obligatory to some Muslims and not all, is because comprehension of it requires a profound authoritative grasp punctuated by a recondite discernment of the Qur'ān, Islām, the worldview of Islām, history and philosophy. Furthermore, this division into two categories:

"Is itself a procedure of doing justice to knowledge and to the man who seeks it, for all of the knowledge of the prerequisites of the first knowledge is good for man, whereas not all of the knowledge of the second kind is good for him; for the man who seeks that latter knowledge, which would bear considerable influence in determining his secular role and position as a citizen, might not necessarily be a good man."[31]

In addition, apart from the Qur'ān being the inspired word of Allāh, in letter as well as in meaning, it is a book outlining the fundamental elements of the worldview of Islām. This in turn necessitates an intellectual grasp of Muslim history and philosophy, some of which predicates an allegorical interpretation (*ta'wīl*) based upon the interpretation of the verses in the Qur'ān which are apparent (*tafsīr*). This does not assume that the interpretation of verses which are apparent is an easy task. One has only to observe the

---

[30] See the article "Ummah perlu kuasai fardu ain, kifayah", published by *Berita Harian*, Monday, the 27th of September 2004, 9.

[31] Syed Muhammad Naquib al-Attas, *Prolegomena*, 73.

voluminous works of the commentators of the Qur'ān (*mufassirūn*), Ibn Kathīr, Fakhr al-Dīn al-Rāzī, and al-Baydāwī, to name a few, to realise that this kind of exercise requires someone who is an authority. But according to the current ideological trend, history and philosophy are no longer relevant. Is this really the case? Or is the current trend with regard to history and philosophy, and Islamic thought in general, a result of ignorance?

The Prime Minister has said that:

> "The Malay society must be a society that embraces knowledge, skills and expertise in order to build capacity. Islam makes it compulsory for Muslims to embrace knowledge in all fields. The misconception that there exists a difference between so-called secular knowledge and religious knowledge must be corrected".[32]

But how are the Malays supposed to embrace knowledge if those entrusted to transmit that knowledge are themselves not qualified, or who are themselves ignorant? Those in the local universities and higher institutions of learning, entrusted with transmitting knowledge beneficial to the condition of man, both in terms of his material and spiritual well being, do not talk much about the Prophet. Consequently, they concentrate their efforts on trying to impose the *sharīʿah*, which is itself reliant upon a thorough

---

[32] See the Prime Minister's keynote address delivered at the UMNO General Assembly on the 23rd of September 2004 in Kuala Lumpur.

understanding of history and philosophy. There is also a tendency to hide behind a presumed authority and quote governmental leaders. This has inevitably led to a loss of identity. A primary example is with the current fervour related to the phrase 'Islam hadhari'. Once again we rely on past Muslim masters to enlighten us on the condition of man. According to them,[33] there are four kinds of people. The first, is one who knows and knows he knows for verily he is a learned, erudite authority (*'ālim*), so adhere to him. Next, is one who knows but is not aware that he knows, verily he is lost, so warn him. The third, is one who knows not but knows he knows not, verily he is ignorant, so teach him. Lastly, he is one who knows not and knows not he knows not, verily he is an imbecile, so distance yourself from him. This characterisation of the kinds of people serves as a warning to those seeking guidance through knowledge. The last mentioned classification implies that the one who knows not, will never admit to it because his bestial nature has taken control of him, thus preventing him from recognising his ignorance. It is not our intention to point an accusing finger at any one particular individual. Suffice it to say however, the intellectual tradition envisioned by the Prime Minister is sadly lacking due in part to a preponderance of those in position of power who are there simply by virtue of 'who they know', and not by virtue of 'what they know'.

Also prevalent in the current ideological milieu, is the government's desire to vigorously promote what is referred

---

[33] We are referring to both al-Ghazzālī and al-Juwaynī in particular.

to as a 'mental revolution'.[34] We will show that this 'revolution' has already begun by using reason and sound philosophical arguments to show that the idea of 'Islam hadhari' as they understand it, is flawed.

---

[34] This idea was recently reintroduced following the republication of the book *Mental Revolution* (Petaling Jaya: Pelanduk Publications, 2004), originally published in the Malay language in 1970 by the UMNO Youth.

FOUR

THE RISE OF PHILOSOPHY
WITHIN THE FRAMEWORK OF THE
WORLDVIEW OF ISLĀM

THE PRIME MINISTER has said, "we must also encourage
reform and renewal in Islamic thought".[1] In order to
exemplify that desire and encourage its passage to fruition, a
brief summary of the role of philosophy in Islamic thought
must be understood.

Historians will agree that history, according to Ibn
Khaldūn, has a dual aspect; the external and the internal.[2]
The distinction between the two becomes manifest only after
having understood the basic meaning and character of
history itself. We may define history as being a narrative

---

[1] See the article "Muslim world needs a meeting of minds", published in the *New Straits Times*, Tuesday, the 5th of October 2004.

[2] The following is derived from the first chapter of Dr. Ali Caksu's
PhD thesis entitled "Causality in History: Ibn Khaldun's and
Hegel's Transformation of Aristotelian Causes", submitted to the
International Institute of Islamic Thought and Civilization
(ISTAC), Kuala Lumpur, February 1999.

dealing with various conditions of social, political, monarchic and dynastic condition. In addition, history may also be defined to include the development and growth, or decline, of the cultural, economic and scientific institutions present in any given civilisation. The former definition refers to the external aspect of history, whereas the latter definition refers to its internal aspect. In order for the external aspect of history to be understood correctly requires that it be presented in an elegant style, a style whereby its narratives must have the ability to garner the attention and approval of large audiences while simultaneously informing the audience of the human condition. Therefore, one may reasonably conclude that in terms of the external aspect, the narrative one refers to as 'history' is an 'art'.

On the other hand, an understanding and appreciation of the internal aspect of history no longer relies on the excellent penmanship, research capabilities or the literary prowess of the historian. It is deeply rooted in speculative thought, logical reasoning and an understanding of the causes of events. Thus it requires a 'philosophic' or 'scientific' interpretation. Hence, one may reasonably conclude that in terms of the internal aspect of history, the narrative one refers to as 'history's in fact a 'science'.

If one were to examine the activities of the past to which one commonly refers to as philosophy,[3] it is possible to

---

[3] The following with regard to the definition of philosophy and the distinction between the worldview of Islām juxtaposed against the Greek and Western worldviews, was extracted from the introduction to my PhD thesis entitled "The Mashshā'ī Philosophical System, A Study, Commentary on and Translation of the Hidāyah

classify all such activities as attempts to apprehend a conceptual understanding of the universe within a system. Therefore, if one were to think of philosophy as a science comprising a study of these systems it would necessarily define philosophy as a science of systems. If one were to take into consideration the fact that there are activities within the study of philosophy which are not directed towards the establishment of systems, activities acute to the evaluation of particular problems within a given system, then the definition of philosophy has to be the science which discusses systems and system related inquiry. The framework for evaluating the process through which philosophy develops into a science as a discipline lends insight into how philosophy evolves in a given society. This clarification also assumes that the rise of a civilisation coincides with the rise of scientific and philosophical activity.

In order to propose a theoretical framework for the rise of a civilisation, one would have to examine that civilisation until the rise of sciences and philosophical activities become evident. The scientific and philosophical activities are particular to each civilisation; differences in each arise as considerations pertaining to culture and periodisation, however, the unifying element among civilisations is the framework through which is found the explanation for the rise of philosophy and science in that civilisation. A worldview, understood in this context to mean the principle formula-

---

al-Ḥikmah of Athīr al-Dīn al-Abharī", albeit with a few minor changes, submitted to the International Institute of Islamic Thought and Civilization (ISTAC), Kuala Lumpur, September 2002.

tions dictating life, enacts a certain dynamism that may begin at the social sphere culminating in a dissemination into all aspects of life. The causes for this dynamism vary greatly among civilisations. However, in general, it is a moral struggle engraved in the very nature of man which in turn motivates society to this conflict. This physical moral struggle leads to a justification of morality through intellectual dynamism and gradually a tradition will be established which will in turn lead to the establishment of a civilisation.

It is clear from this very abstract framework that the 'rise' and 'decline' of a civilisation is dependant upon this intellectual dynamism punctuated by philosophy and philosophical thought. With more and more intellectual ideas coming into being, so too an accumulation of knowledge. This leads to an inevitable shift with regard to certain conceptions of the mind. Out of these certain fundamentals are questioned and their solutions give rise to yet more inquiry until conclusions are reached that point to the importance of intellectual endeavour and the establishment of schools. Such circles of scholarly activity are necessary, because in order for scientific and philosophical activities to become institutionalised, a tradition is required. This tradition then becomes an integral part of society. This framework, though abstract, can be generally described as the antecedent by which the Western and, to a certain extent, the Greek civilisations emerged. Differences, however, become apparent when comparisons between their respective worldviews are analysed.

One can say that the Greek worldview in particular developed out of a natural worldview, one where simplistic notions of the world dealing only with phenomenal occurrences were viewed as the underlying principles of being and man's purpose as a whole. As such, it was the culture that determined the direction of the worldview so that throughout its history, that worldview may be perfected and moulded accordingly. Were the origins of Greek philosophy born of necessity, out of an overwhelming curiosity to explain how things are? If one were to accept this to be factual, it is not possible to explain why the study of the nature of things be assigned exclusively to the Greeks. If one were to argue that although the study of nature was carried out by other peoples as well, but that somehow the Greeks were the only ones who studied the nature of things in such a way that it gradually led to the development of sciences, one can reasonably infer that there must have been at least two ways utilised for the study of nature. Firstly, a 'scientific' study that led to the emergence of the sciences; secondly, one that did not lead to the emergence of any sciences, but occurred merely out of man's inherent curiosity to know. However, this explanation is superfluous as far as method is concerned, and therefore a further elucidation justifying the exclusivity of Greek scholasticism is warranted. Therefore it is possible, based on the premise that a moral dynamism which found its genesis in the social sphere culminating in the intellectual sphere, that long before the acclaimed first philosopher Thales, there were activities influenced by an intellectual environment that led to his 'scientific' or 'natural' studies. Based upon this premise, it is theorised that the moral dynamism referred to may have had its roots in mythological epics. The romance of these epics contain, apart from the more obvious literal inferences, allegorical suppositions of morality and of man's struggle with his self, and of temptation and will, orchestrated by a pantheon of gods. Being triumphant over the gods inhabiting nature meant therefore, that man alone would dictate his destiny in which case freedom could be achieved.

In general, one may postulate the Western worldview to have developed historically. What we mean is that the worldview is shaped by a series of successive intellectual traditions each typified by the ideological milieu, derived "from cultural and philosophical elements aided by the science of their times".[4] Therefore, the fundamental elements of such a worldview are necessarily impermanent, dependant upon the persistent formulation of new ideologies. Consequently, the worldview is in a constant state of 'becoming', never actually achieving maturity and therefore cannot be "conscious of its own identity".[5] In truth, it was the appearance of Islām that guided the West away from its intellectual wasteland causing revolutionary changes which would leave a permanent imprint not only on Christianity, by allowing it to assume the guise of a 'revealed' religion, but also on the different schools of thought which would then participate in the shaping of its worldview.[6]

---

[4] *Prolegomena*, 4.

[5] Ibid., 4.

[6] For a detailed exposition on the roots of Western intellectualism and the corruption of the term 'revealed' as applied to Christianity, please see Syed Muhammad Naquib al-Attas, *Islām and Secularism* (Kuala Lumpur: International Institute of Islamic Thought and Civilization (ISTAC), 1993). Henceforth cited as *Islām and Secularism*.

Indeed Aristotelianism, or rationalism, would become the ideological premise upon which subsequent ideologies were formulated. This adoption in itself was revolutionary, not so much because it led to the systematic establishment of schools dedicated to scholarly inquiry instrumental in the shaping of Western history leading to the dramatically familiar 'revolution' in the sciences, but more because it threatened radical changes fundamental to the established foundations of Christianity. How to reconcile the problems between reason and revelation, the One and the many, of movement and change, the Word and the laws of Nature, were problems aimed at the very core of religion. Their solution, founded with the aid of rationalism, presented itself in the form of the theory of twofold truths, permanently establishing a dichotomy between the sacred and the profane. The most conspicuous problem resulting from this dichotomy however, is the problem of knowledge because a conviction resulting from one could form a necessary preliminary attack on the other.

From this brief assertion it becomes clear that the Greek and Western worldviews "formed gradually through a historical and developmental process of philosophical speculation and scientific discovery",[7] one in which man occupies a central position. This is not the case however from the perspective of the worldview of Islām.

Unlike the Greek and Western worldviews, the worldview of Islām is not one born out of culture, or social dilemma; conversely it is the worldview that determines and

---

[7] *Prolegomena*, 2.

gives rise to culture, and consequently civilisation. Nor is it founded upon a dynamism punctuated by "philosophical speculation formulated mainly from observation of the data of sensible experience, of what is visible to the eye; nor is it restricted to *kawn*, which is the world of sensible experience, the world of created things".[8] It is not one where the foundations for its worldview are deeply rooted in the rise of the sciences, whose premises are based solely on an immersion with the phenomenal world, its fate at the mercy of ideological paradigms,[9] nor is it receptive of the dichotomy between the sacred and the profane, or described by historical periodisation. "What is meant by 'worldview' according to the perspective of Islām, is then the vision of reality and truth that appears before our mind's eye revealing what existence is all about; for it is the world of existence in its totality that Islām is projecting".[10] The source for this vision of reality and truth is Revelation which projects the fundamental elements of the worldview; elements whose

---

[8] Ibid, 1.

[9] We are referring to the Kuhnian interpretation of paradigm and paradigm shift. See Thomas S. Kuhn, *The Structure of Scientific Revolutions* (Chicago: The University of Chicago Press, 1970), 2nd ed. Here Kuhn proposes that while the passage of science is largely influenced by the nonrational and a preponderance of a certain intellectual ideology supported by concomitant methodology, which give rise to more complex theories than those preceding them, these new theories however, are not representative of being any closer to the truth as viewed rationally. It is these new more complex theories that are representative of paradigms.

[10] *Prolegomena*, 2.

knowledge is based on certainty.[11] We have already made a general reference with regard to the rise of the sciences in the preceding paragraphs when we referred to both the Greek and Western conceptions of worldview and the subsequent rise of the sciences. We have mentioned that it resulted from man's overwhelming desire to know primarily about God, His creation, existence, the nature of the soul and so forth, and then to explain how things are. Since we maintain that both the Greek and Western worldviews deny Revealed knowledge, logically then, there are no fundamental elements as such, and therefore this explanation assumes that man's inquiry proceeds from what he does not know and then tries to explain the unknown employing empirical methods and aided by reason alone. However, the arrival of knowledge of the Absolute cannot be attained through reason alone and consequently certainty is in doubt. This doubt is receptive of speculation. Prior knowledge then becomes suspect while new theories and ideas are formulated resulting in new knowledge which in turn admits doubt. Hence, knowledge which is not impregnable to doubt cannot therefore constitute certitude. From this assertion, it becomes immediately clear that the worldview of Islām does not suffer from the problem of knowledge. Revelation does not stand in opposition to the faculty of reason, nor is reason incapable of grasping the truths of Revelation. Indeed, the fundamental elements projected by Revelation and aided by

---

[11] For a complete definition and understanding of the reference to the term certainty (*yaqīn*), see Syed Muhammad Naquib al-Attas, *Islām and Secularism*, 86, 135 n. 112.

the interpretations and demonstrations of the Prophet reveals the essence of Islamic sciences.

The pervading opinion dominating Western sciences is that the Islamic sciences in general are nothing more than perhaps a continuation of the Greek sciences and that Muslim philosophers are mere transmitters of earlier Greek masters. This opinion assumes that Islamic sciences developed independently of revealed knowledge and that Muslim philosophers had nothing new to offer nor did they contribute to 'revolutionary' thought. This opinion further assumes that such a thing referred to as Islamic sciences did not and could not exist, which would then lead one to conclude that the intellectual milieu was one of stagnancy and incapacity. Factual evidence for this and other deriding opinions concerning Muslim achievements does not exist. The immutable axis of revealed doctrine, not to mention intuitive knowledge confirmed by revelation, certainly bisected the Greek civilisation. Therefore, the resemblance between Greek and Muslim sciences cannot be assumed to be purely a complete adoption of the former by the latter.[12] Hence, the supposition that Muslim masters borrowed everything from the Greeks is erroneous, although we agree that they did borrow some wisdom from the Ancient philosophies. The following *ḥadīth* of the Prophet Muḥammad (peace be upon him) is a true testimony to the ability of Islām to borrow from other civilisations, if the knowledge

---

[12] See also Titus Burckhardt, *Mirror of the Intellect* (Albany: State University of New York Press, 1987), 18-19.

contained therein does not run counter to the truths demonstrated by Islām:

"Abū Hurayrah (Allāh be pleased with him) reported Allāh's messenger (pbuh) as saying: a word of wisdom is the lost property of a believer, he can take it wherever he finds it, because he is more entitled to it."[13]

In addition, if certain elements within the Greek philosophical system were understood by Muslims to be antithetical and in opposition to the fundamental elements of the worldview of Islām, these elements were either discarded or were transformed by the application of religious philosophy (*kalām*) in order that those ideas conform to distinctive principles within the fundamental elements of the worldview of Islām.[14] Conversely, if one were to assume the supposition to be true, what then defines science as understood in Islām? What element differentiates it from the Greek sciences? What is it that makes it distinct?

The centuries prior to the appearance of Ḥujjat al-Islām Abū Ḥāmid Muḥammad ibn Muḥammad ibn Muḥammad al-Ghazzālī al-Ṭūsī (450-505H/1058-1111CE) mentioned by the Prime Minister in his poetic composition, and who is

---

[13] Sunan al-Tirmidhī, *Kitāb al-'Ilm, al-Kutub al-Sittah wa Shurūḥuhā*, bāb 19, ḥadīth 2687 (Istanbul: Cagri, 1992).

[14] These ideas are briefly discussed by Cemil Akdoğan, "Muslim Influence upon European Scholarship and Learning", (*Al-Shajarah*, Journal of the International Institute of Islamic Thought and Civilization (ISTAC), 2001), v.6, n.2, 161-196. See also Alnoor Dhanani, *Muslim Philosophy and The Sciences* (The Muslim Almanac, New York: Gale Research Inc., 1996), 190.

mentioned in the following chapter, accompanied by the intellectual zest and material splendour of the Muslim world, produced a corpus of philosophical and scientific knowledge which was to leave a permanent seal upon Western civilisation more than any other civilisation before or since. The pivotal dilemma facing the Muslim philosophers before the appearance of al-Ghazzālī was how to reconcile God's absolute unity and perfection with the multiplicity of creation without postulating a duality in Him. These same problems confounded the Greeks from Aristotle to Plotinus. Although Muslim philosophers accepted many of the Aristotelian postulates giving them due acknowledgement, they did not develop them merely as continuations from Greek thought devoid of new ideas expressed in the same doctrinal manner of the *Logos* or *Nous* in order to succumb to the demands of logical reasoning alone. On the contrary, new ideas and interpretations were afforded which both satisfied the demands of reason and did not violate the teachings of the Qur'ān. In this regard, Muslim philosophers managed to formulate a new system quite distinct from that of their Greek predecessors.

In addition, the language of the Qur'ān and its message had now enriched the language of philosophy. For example, logic derived essentially from Aristotle was of a nature described by the Ten Categories in which substance was the definitive reality of existence. It was unable to prove the truths pertaining to God or the machinations of the First Cause. Aristotelian philosophy could not then prove the unity of God, His Oneness, and had no conception of His attributes. Solutions to these problems were developed in part by Muslim philosophy and answered by the worldview of Islām. We have already mentioned that the genesis of Islamic sciences resulted from inquiry into the fundamental elements of the worldview projected by Revelation. Such an inquiry, in order for it to be called 'islamic', must involve the "liberation of man first from magical, mythological, animistic, national-cultural tradition opposed to Islām, and then from secular control over his reason and his language".[15] This liberation is known as *islamisation*,[16] and refers primarily to the return of man "towards perfection in his progress towards realisation of his original nature as spirit".[17] In addition, paramount to the process of islamisation is:

"... the islamisation of language, and this fact is demonstrated by the Holy Qur'ān itself when it was first revealed among the Arabs. Language, thought and reason are closely interconnected and are indeed interdependent in projecting to man his worldview or vision of reality."[18]

---

[15] *Islām and Secularism*, 44.

[16] Ibid. Al-Attas is the originator of the concept of islamisation. The term has been much in vogue in recent times and has received widespread acclaim as one of the most fundamental concepts central to the understanding of the current dilemma facing the Muslims and their apparent backwardness with regard to the sciences in particular. See also Wan Mohd. Nor Wan Daud, *The Educational Philosophy and Practice of Syed Muhammad Naquib al-Attas; an Exposition of the Original Concept of Islamization* (Kuala Lumpur: International Institute of Islamic Thought and Civilization (ISTAC), 1998).

[17] Ibid., 45.

[18] Ibid.

Basic ontological questions concerning man and his role, the epistemological issues concerning God as Universal being and the Source of all knowledge were at once immediately answered by the Holy Qur'ān.[19] It is clear then that the Arabic language experienced a transformation, not in terms of its systematic combination of roots, or form, but in terms of meaning, or matter. For instance, in pre-islamic Arabia, the term *kāfir* was used to indicate one who was ungrateful to a gracious host. Islām, however, islamised the term to mean one who denies Islām.[20]

Similarly, Muslim philosophy, in interpreting new ideas, was aided by the language of the Qur'ān which afforded

---

[19] Al-'Alaq/96: 1-5. See also Wan Mohd. Nor Wan Daud, *The Educational Philosophy and Practice of Syed Muhammad Naquib al-Attas; an Exposition of the Original Concept of Islamization* (Kuala Lumpur: International Institute of Islamic Thought and Civilization (ISTAC), 1998), 317. The author offers a brief yet profound historical perspective of the islamisation of knowledge. Refer also to chapter one, in particular pages 36-37.

[20] This example was explained to me by Syed Muhammad Naquib al-Attas. This very poignant example points to the fact that once Islamic elements are introduced into the language their meanings take on a whole new dimension. It also clearly speaks to the fact that the Arabic language is the only "divinely inspired living language and is in that sense 'new' and perfected to the superlative degree so that it—especially its basic Islamic vocabulary—is not subject to change and development nor governed by the vicissitudes of social change as in the case of all other languages which derive from culture and tradition". See Syed Muhammad Naquib al-Attas, *Islām and Secularism*, 46. In the above example, reference to the profane now adopts a new meaning directed toward the sacred. It also points to the importance of language in conveying correct meaning and the ability of the Arabic language to adopt new meaning while at the same time retaining its original form.

new terminology quite distinct from Greek terminology both in form and contextual meaning. This did not mean however, that Greek terminology was completely replaced by Quranic language, for the Greek terms which had become arabicised, were still very much a part of Muslim philosophical sciences. The question one must ask however is to what extent did these arabicised terms influence the sciences; were their meanings the same as those understood in Greek both in contextual meaning and form? In the preceding paragraphs, we have made reference to the fact that the genesis of Muslim sciences resulted from the fundamental elements of the worldview of Islām. The worldview itself must possess language reflective of Islām and its fundamental elements and hence, the sciences, in order for them to be termed 'Islamic' or 'Muslim', must necessarily possess that same reflective language. Muslim philosophers were very careful to develop a system whereby it could not be assumed that the use of Greek terminology meant the adoption of those same ideas. Indeed some elements of Greek philosophy were adopted by Muslims if, in fact, their suppositions were not opposed to the worldview of Islām. So who were these Muslim masters? They are the subject of our next chapter.

FIVE

AL-GHAZZĀLĪ AND THE INTELLECTUAL
MILIEU PRECEDING HIM

THE SIGNIFICANCE OF the Prime Minister's poetic composition referred to at the onset of this book represents the
primary source in our attempt to connect the ideas contained
therein, with the much in vogue phrase 'Islam hadhari', the
explanation of which by the various relevant 'authorities' we
find to be grossly inadequate. Suffice it to say however, our
treatment of the latter explanation to be discussed in the
following chapter, represents the earliest attempt to adequately comprehend, analyse and suggest a definition for it
in its true meaning as envisioned by the Prime Minister. One
point worthy of mention, in reference to the Prime
Minister's poetic composition, is the fact that this is the first
time in the annals of the Malaysian political arena that such
an inspired poem indicating an intellectual approach is thrust
to the fore. Never before has a Prime Minister of Malaysia
invoked the names of al-Ghazzālī or al-Shāfiʿī in such a

manner. Never before has a leader of an Asian nation submitted to the authority of one who stands out prominently as the most representative spirit of his era. Why do we feel the need to offer a summary of the intellectual milieu preceding al-Ghazzālī? Would not this kind of exercise appear more relevant to the discipline of Islamic thought and not the political arena? What we are trying to elucidate is the connection between the genesis of ideas and their relevance leading up to the time al-Ghazzālī flourished, and that which led to al-Ghazzālī being hailed as the greatest scholar of Islām. We take particular note of the fact that the earlier generations of Muslim scholars adopted some of the ideas postulated by the ancients, modified those ideas deemed antithetical to the worldview of Islām in light of Quranic edification, and then proceeded to integrate them to conform to that teaching. Some of those modified ideas may be considered original since their purpose and meaning was now indicative of an Islamic framework. However, as we shall see:

"Certain thought systems and thought orientations [which] were adopted from outside sources (not necessarily wholly antagonistic to the Qur'ān but certainly alien to and not infrequently incompatible with it), adapted somewhat to the Islamic mental milieu, and [were] expressed mostly in Islamic terminology, but this thin veneer could not hide the fact that their basic structure of ideas was not drawn from within the Qur'ān itself."[1]

This condition prepared the stage for al-Ghazzālī's eventual appearance. His mastery in terms of comprehending and interpreting the verses of the Qur'ān which were both apparent and allegorical, of exegesis, and extraordinary genius in comprehending both Greek ideas and those of their followers from amongst the Muslim philosophers, effectively made him the representative of Islamic orthodoxy in spite of its many weaknesses.

Therefore, in order to paint a picture of the intellectual milieu preceding al-Ghazzālī and to indicate his place in the Islamic philosophical tradition, we feel it necessary to present a brief summary of the socio-political and intellectual atmosphere of the preceding centuries, in particular the period between the ninth century until the time of al-Ghazzālī. However, in doing so, I have not conducted an exhaustive summary of all the thinkers and literary figures known to have lived during the period mentioned, for two reasons. Firstly, the order of prolixity will probably result in more conflict rather than resolve on the part of the reader; secondly, in general the ideas discussed during this period do not differ much in terms of matter until the time of Ibn Sīnā, hence, to elaborate on each and every idea would be redundant. Therefore, in order to preserve the themes central to the following discussion we select only those prominent

---

[1] Fazlur Rahman, *Islam and Modernity* (Chicago and London: The University of Chicago Press, 1984), 3.

figures which have become synonymous with the Islamic sciences in general, and with philosophy in particular.

Indeed, prior to the rise of Islām, the pursuit of intellectualism was somewhat centred around the task of translating a number of Greek philosophical texts into Syriac and later into Arabic. This was already being done by Nestorian Christians in both Syria and Persia where centres of learning were established. By the middle of the eighth century, these centres of learning began to receive patronage by the 'Abbāsid caliphs, who had by this time, established Baghdad as their capital.[2] Caliph al-Ma'mūn, in particular, was responsible for the founding of *Bayt al-Ḥikmah*, a research institute serving as the primary axis for the transmission of translated works. At the time medical and astronomical texts were of primary interest which was perhaps partly due to the fact that many translators were employed as physicians to the caliph as well. In addition, a number of Platonic dialogues, including the *Timaeus*, Euclid's *Elements* and Ptolemy's *Almagest* were among the translated works. Two centuries later virtually nothing remained as far as the work of translations for "almost the entire corpus of Greek medicine, natural philosophy and mathematical science had been rendered into usable Arabic versions."[3]

---

[2] See David Lindberg, *The Beginnings of Western Science: The European Scientific Tradition in Philosophical, Religious, and Institutional Context, 600 B.C. to A.D. 1450* (Chicago: The University of Chicago Press, 1992), 168.

[3] Ibid., 170. For a recent summary of the translation activity, see Dimitri Gutas, "Aspects of Literary Form and Genre in Arabic Logical Works", in Charles Burnett (ed.), *Glosses and Commen-*

The following thinkers lived within the shadow of the age of splendour during the rule of the 'Abbāsid caliphs. We are reminded in the elegantly portrayed narratives of the *Thousand and One Nights* of the economic wealth, literary wit, cultural splendour and political upheavals. Although perhaps much of the descriptions of the times were exaggerated to suit the powers that held sway, what we are interested in is the intellectual milieu surrounding that culture. The period of the *Thousand and One Nights* may be referred to as the "exotic paradigm",[4] in large part due to the descriptions contained in those narratives complete with unabashed flattery and entertaining wit. However, the reality, referred to as "the paradigm of patronage, was an uneasy symbiosis between artist and court patron".[5] The artist was essentially at the mercy, whim and good graces of his patron. Depending on the latter's humours, the former was either held in high esteem or was banished to the point of destitution, or worse. Conversely, the skill of the artist or literary man was such that he saw opportunity in shameless flattery. This was frequently the case with al-Mutanabbī (915-965CE), the renowned poet who would often resort to fits of poetic genius in order that his patron's purse strings be relaxed, simply by clever manipulation, flattery and an acute sense of his patron's shortcomings, or more precisely

---

taries on Aristotelian Logical Texts (London: The Warburg Institute, University of London, 1993), 29-76.
[4] Ian Richard Netton, *Al-Fārābī and His School* (London and New York: Routledge, 1992), 19.
[5] Ibid., 21.

his vanities, which he would then use to his favour.[6] Then there is the "ideal paradigm",[7] a phase where there was mutual respect between the learned and patron, not simply due to monetary incentive but rather an actual concerted effort to advance the cause of learning. The ninth century was a period of intellectual ferment; it was a time of translations. The ideologically opposed arguments concerning philosophy and *kalām* were in infancy, and the controversies posited by Mu'tazilism had the political ear of the 'Abbāsid caliph. These controversies concerned matters of theology between both the "patterns of tradition (*naql*) and reason (*'aql*)".[8] It would appear that each tradition adhered to an established ideology which could neither share any common features between them nor agree to disagree. Abū Yūsuf Ya'qūb b. Ishāq al-Kindī (185-256/ 801-870) emerged as the first thinker in Islām to attempt an ideological synthesis between the two. It comes as no surprise then that he founded a school which combined the sciences with philosophy. Born in Basra, the scion of noble Arab lineage from the tribe of Kindah, he was afforded the best education possible. Influence from the school of Jundīshāpūr, made famous by the Bakhtishū family, was perhaps the impetus for his interest toward learning. Al-Kindī was opposed to the Greek idea with regard to both the eternity of the world and the rationalist assumption that

---

[6] Ibid., 21-22.

[7] Ibid., 25.

[8] Mustafa Ceric, *Roots of Synthetic Theology in Islām: A Study of the Theology of Abū Manṣūr al-Māturīdī* (Kuala Lumpur: International Institute of Islamic Thought and Civilization, 1995), 25.

nothing begets nothing.[9] In relation to the former opposition, he would often resort to the authority of the Qur'ān as a source of proof,[10] while in terms of the latter assumption, al-Kindī accepted the Neoplatonic emanationist theory conditionally asserting a created first being *ex nihilo* through the act of God, a significant departure from the Aristotelian conception.[11] This points to the fact that from the very beginning, al-Kindī in particular, and later on the Muslim philosopher in general, could not be thought of as being a mere transmitter of Greek thought. Al-Attas explains:

> "Al-Kindī's remark in the book addressed to al-Mu'taṣim, that he wanted to complete what the Greek philosophers did not fully express, points to the fact that the Muslim thinkers did not look upon the Greek philosophers from the position of imitators; on the contrary, even though they respected them for their rational endeavour and achievements, they at the same time saw their errors and inadequacy in arriving at knowledge about the ultimate nature of reality through the effort of reason alone."[12]

---

[9] See for instance Majid Fakhry, *A History of Islamic Philosophy* (New York: Columbia University Press, 1983), 69. In fact al-Kindī was opposed not only to the doctrine of the eternity of the world and the denial of creation *ex nihilo*, but also to the impossibility of bodily resurrection, the impossibility of miracles and the view that knowledge derived from prophetic revelation was invalid.

[10] *Roots of Synthetic Theology in Islām: A Study of the Theology of Abū Manṣūr al-Māturīdī*, 26.

[11] *A History of Islamic Philosophy*, 69.

[12] The preceding quotation is from Professor Dr. Syed Muhammad Naquib al-Attas' welcoming address to participants of the International Conference on al-Ghazzālī's Legacy: Its Contemporary

The conception of knowledge, he declared, was of two kinds; divine knowledge (*al-'ilm al-ilāhī*) and human knowledge (*al-'ilm al-insānī*), the former being of a superior degree only given to prophets. Revealed truths at this level are self evident and as such cannot be receptive of demonstration. Within the context of human knowledge however, there are different degrees the most superior form being philosophy. Truths at this level may be grasped by human intelligence and, as such, are receptive of demonstration. Similarly, al-Kindī divides the sciences into two categorics: divine science (*al-'ilm al-ilāhī*), and human sciences (*al-'ulūm al-insāniyyah*). By virtue of the fact that divine knowledge is only given to prophets, divine science is only possessed by prophets.

Let us now turn our attention to al-Kindī's division of philosophy which is constructed around the various modes of human knowledge. The primary mode is that of sense experience, through which the faculties of the senses apprehend external objects. This apprehension however is impermanent and requires the representative faculty, in which a perceived object is preserved temporarily as a mental form before being committed to the retentive faculty, which then preserves its meaning. This primary mode is limited only to sensible particulars. Intelligible universals are known through rational cognition. Truths apprehended at this level and perceived through the faculty of reason are *a priori*; in

---

Relevance, held from the 24th-27th of October 2002 at the International Institute of Islamic Thought and Civilization (ISTAC), Kuala Lumpur.

other words, truths which are intuitively known.[13] For rational cognition, the object of perception is the universal which is immaterial and therefore neither a representation of it nor a sense image corresponding to the phenomenological world, is possible. Immaterial entities as such are apprehended intellectually.[14] This distinction between the material and the immaterial serves as a propaedeutic to al-Kindī's conception of philosophy. According to him, there are two aspects of philosophy; physics, and metaphysics, the latter of which is also referred to as first philosophy (*al-falsafah al-ūlā*). Both aspects are also called "the science of the movable and the immovable respectively",[15] and "the science of the divine and created things".[16] Fakhry states that "he appears to simplify the Aristotelian formula by recognising

---

[13] Al-Kindī, "Kitāb al-Kindī ilā al-Mu'taṣim billāh fi'l falsafah al-ūlā", *Rasā'il al-Kindī al-Falsafiyyah*, 107-109. The classification of the senses according to al-Kindī was later elaborated further by Ibn Sīnā. He discussed at great length the faculties of the senses which was instrumental in the development of his psychology and was ultimately reflected in his ontology. See also Majid Fakhry, *A History of Islamic Philosophy*, 71-72.

[14] Some immaterial entities may "be associated with matter accidentally, and this might give rise to the illusion that they are susceptible of representation. Such, for instance, is the case with shape, which exists in conjunction with matter, and is nevertheless a purely rational concept, arrived at by abstraction and independently from the sensible object in which it inheres". Al-Kindī, "Kitāb al-Kindī ilā al-Mu'taṣim billāh fi'l falsafah al-ūlā", *Rasā'il al-Kindī al-Falsafiyyah*, 108. See also, *A History of Islamic Philosophy*, 72.

[15] *A History of Islamic Philosophy*, 72.

[16] Ibid., the former referring to metaphysics, the latter to physics.

two against Aristotle's three theoretical sciences".[17] However, in our opinion, another possibility exists; namely, that al-Kindī is following the Quranic interpretation of things having a dual aspect, an outer (*zāhir*) and an inner (*bātin*) aspect.

Earlier we considered the fact that al-Kindī postulates knowledge of having two aspects, divine and human. In connection to this, we have also mentioned the science of philosophy as having two aspects, both of which are receptive of demonstration (*burhān*). However, with regard to metaphysics, or first philosophy which is defined as knowledge of The First Real-True One (*al-Wāhid al-Haqq al-Awwal*), by virtue of its being the cause of all Reality, demonstration cannot rely on rational propositions alone and must therefore transcend to the level of self-evident truths. This implies that unlike the Greek conception of knowledge which denies Revealed knowledge and relies principally on definitions arrived at through reason alone and then applied to all sciences equally, al-Kindī's conception relies on definition, sometimes arrived at through reason, while at other times through revealed knowledge.

On God, al-Kindī considers Him to be the First Real True One and the Eternal (*al-Qadīm*), the First Principle of all things. This One is not one conceived to be receptive of addition and subtraction, generation and corruption, a composite for this would assume the predication of a genus and a differentia, or contained within a clearly defined set of boundaries. Nor is it one predicated of a genus and species,

---

[17] Ibid.

or of non-existence and a cause other than itself, because God as such cannot be predicated of any created thing. He is not receptive of change otherwise that would imply that He is predicated of a genus which is impossible. Yet there is a contradiction with his conception of God. Earlier we have considered that al-Kindī argues for creation *ex nihilo* by the sheer act of Creation, yet God is conceived as being Necessary. The act of Creation implies that God must possess power, wisdom and will. However, being Necessary denies God a will and this is where the contradiction lies.[18]

Al-Kindī's cosmological scheme is based in part on his opposition to the premise that a body could be infinite. If, he argues, one were to remove a finite part from an infinite whole, then that which remains must either be infinite or finite, but one already assumes the whole to be infinite. Therefore, when the finite part is conjoined once again to the infinite whole, the resultant body would either be greater or equal to its original magnitude. If the former is assumed, this would imply that infinite bodies are unequal whereas if the latter were assumed, this would imply that both the part and the whole are equal.[19] This kind of argument employing the use of exceptive syllogism built upon conjunctive and disjunctive propositions extends to al-Kindī's opposition to

---

[18] This position would later be adopted by, in particular, Ibn Sīnā who refers to God as Necessary Agent. Al-Ghazzālī argues in his *Tahāfut* that this is in fact a contradiction in terms, employing logical premise to show that Ibn Sīnā uses terms which are mutually exclusive.

[19] Al-Kindī, "Kitāb al-Kindī ilā al-Mu'taṣim billāh fi'l falsafah al-ūlā", *Rasā'il al-Kindī al-Falsafiyyah*, 114. See also, *A History of Islamic Philosophy*, 74.

the idea of infinite time, space and motion. We do not need to concern ourselves here with an exhaustive elaboration of al-Kindī's ideas. We need only mention that he was by no means of the opinion that philosophy was superior to, or even on par with, revelation. He acknowledged the superiority of the Qur'ān, that philosophy "should simply surrender its claims to be the highest pathway to truth and be willing to subordinate itself as an ancillary to revelation".[20]

In the tenth century (4th century AH), Muslim theologians (*mutakallimūn*) came to view Greek philosophy as suspect, as a way of thinking that seemed particularly alien. The intrusion of Greek logic and the Peripatetic sciences which sought to perceive a necessary nexus between cause and effect threatened Divine sovereignty. Any necessity posited for the created order was rejected by many Muslim theologians; accordingly, many embraced the Quranic interpretation of creation and causality which saw events in the created world as the acts of the one universal God. He alone is the true cause of all that happens. The position which these Muslim theologians feared can be found in the works of Abū Naṣr Muḥammad b. Muḥammad b. Tarkhān b. Uzlūgh al-Fārābī (258-339H/870-950CE) and al-Shaykh al-Ra'īs Abū 'Alī al-Ḥusayn Ibn Sīnā (370-428H/980-1037CE) which epitomises the antithesis of the views of the theologians. Al-Fārābī, for instance, established a curriculum devoted to the study of Plato and Aristotle, while the works of Ibn Sīnā, particularly in natural philosophy and metaphysics, wielded extraordinary influence. Clearly the path in

---

[20] *A History of Islamic Philosophy*, 91.

which Greek philosophical thought found its way into the Islamic world can be attributed to the works of these two masters.[21]

Al-Fārābī by all accounts was undoubtedly the most legendary philosopher, logician, linguist, and musician; such was his fame, due in large part to the wide influence his writings had later in the West. The attraction for him follows a trail of near mythic proportions. Much about the facts concerning his life, as described by historians and admirers through the ages, has undoubtedly been exaggerated, and only served to sensationalise his life well beyond the boundaries of historical truth. Consequently, and due in part to the difficulty of separating fact from fiction, much of the truth concerning his life remains mysterious. This apparent difficulty however does not in any way repudiate the magnitude of his intellectual achievements enshrined in the many works composed by him.[22]

Al-Fārābī's expertise in logic is perhaps a reflection of his teachers, one of whom was the Nestorian Christian philosopher Abū Bishr Mattā ibn Yūnus (d. 940CE).[23] His

---

[21] See Ian Richard Netton, *Al-Fārābī and his School* (Routledge: London and New York, 1992).

[22] Ibid., 4.

[23] During his time there appears to have been a debate concerning the merits of logic and Grammar. Abū Bishr maintained that logic is prior and superior to grammar. He was of the opinion that "the logician has no need for it (i.e. grammar) while the grammarian is very much in need of logic. For logic investigates the meaning, while grammar investigates the utterance. If therefore, the logician comes across the utterance this is a mere accident. Likewise, it is by sheer accident that the grammarian stumbles upon the meaning. And the meaning is nobler than the utterance, and the utterance is

place in terms of contribution to the sciences has been firmly established by virtue of his expertise, thorough understanding and elucidation of logic. One of Abū Bishr Mattā ibn Yūnus' basic postulates concerning logic dealt with the difference between logic and grammar. He taught that logic and grammar were different; logic concerns itself with meaning, while grammar considers utterances.[24] For the Muslim logician, it was more a question of priority or superiority of the one over the other.

In terms of al-Fārābī's epistemology, his classification of knowledge is twofold: namely, that which embraces the corporeal and that which addresses the non-corporeal. However, there is a third aspect; that which cannot be known, which can only be described in terms of what a thing is not.[25] The key, however, to al-Fārābī's epistemology lies in his sixfold division of reason ('aql), which for him is synonymous with intellect. The first division, is moral prudence, a faculty characteristic of one whose actions are

---

humbler than the meaning." A reply to this statement came from the philologist Abū Sa'īd al-Sīrāfī (d. 932CE) according to whom, "meanings are not transferable from one language to another but are bound up with utterances...Logic is one aspect of language. Both logic and grammar treat utterances. Logic is the right structure of language. Thus, since logic is understood as the 'logic of language', there is a 'logic of Arabic', and a 'logic of the Greeks'. But there is no universal logic any more than there is a universal grammar or universal language". See Joel L. Kraemer, *Humanism in the Renaissance of Islam* (Leiden: E. J. Brill, 1986), 112-113.

[24] See Joel L. Kraemer, *Humanism in the Renaissance of Islam* (Leiden: E. J. Brill, 1986), 114-115.

[25] Ibid., 40.

directed toward doing good.[26] This is followed by common sense, which is further enhanced by the third division, the faculty of natural perception, described as:

"The faculty of the soul which enables man to grasp the certainty (*al-yaqīn*) of some basic universal and necessary true principles. The faculty derives not from analogy or logical skills or thought but from one's own nature or, at the very least, arises in one's youth ... Man is ignorant of from where or how this reason comes ... it is a part of the soul (*juz' mā min al-nafs*)."[27]

The fourth faculty, also associated with the soul and similar to the first faculty, is described as the voice of conscience, the faculty by which good and evil is known to man.[28] The fifth is subdivided again into four; first, the Potential Intellect. This is the capacity of abstracting the essences of forms of the objects of perception. These abstracted forms are thus the essences existing in the mind. This conception appears to bear some similarities with al-Kindī's definition of rational cognition.[29] Second, The Actual Intellect. This bears a connection to the first in that it is the representation of the essences of forms corresponding to them in reality. However, as long as the object of perception is non-existent, its essence remains as an intellect in potentiality. The Acquired Intellect, the third subdivision, is

---

[26] Ibid., 46.
[27] Ibid., 47.
[28] Ibid.
[29] See footnote 13.

able to comprehend "intelligibles abstracted from matter by the former Reason as well as the immaterial forms which this acquired Reason apprehends immediately".[30] The fourth subdivision, The Agent or Active Intellect is identical with the emanationist Tenth Intellect. The Agent Intellect is free from both matter and form and will never be associated with either. It "is that principle which makes that essence which was an intellect in potentiality, an intellect in actuality, and which makes the intelligibles which are intelligibles in potentiality, intelligibles in actuality".[31] The sixth, and final faculty in his division of reason, is the First Principle (*al-'Aql al-Awwal*), and this leads into his ontology.

Essentially, the First Principle or, First Being or, the One, generates everything in a continuous everlasting process of emanation. It is conceived as being Necessary, without partner, immaterial and undefined. Since it is not associated with matter, it must be Intellect. The act of intellection by the First Being of itself, gives rise to the first emanation, which "is capable of conceiving both its author and itself".[32] The ability of the first intellect to conceive of its author, gives rise to the second intellect, known as the outermost heaven.[33] The successive series of emanations by virtue of the prior intellect having the capability of conceiving of its cause, terminates at the tenth intellect, and with each successive emanation of intellects the more elemental they become, the most basal being the terrestrial region. The

---

[30] *Al-Fārābī and his School*, 49.
[31] Ibid.
[32] *A History of Islamic Philosophy*, 118.
[33] Ibid.

cycle of development now reverses, the hierarchical pattern going from the most basal, prime matter, to the most noble, man.[34] It is clear from his conception of God, and from the theory of emanation fashioned after the Neo-Platonists, that unlike al-Kindī, who we remember conceived of God as being Necessary yet at the same time believed in the act of creation, al-Fārābī's conception was that the world was eternal, in essence denying God a will. "Necessary" meant that something in potentiality must become actualised simultaneously and therefore, the world must be eternal. This idea was certainly adopted from Aristotelian philosophy, which dictates the eternity of the world based on such a premise.

In addressing the faculties of man, al-Fārābī tacitly weaves "the conception of Reason as a faculty of cognition in man".[35] Admitted as "the ultimate pathway to happiness",[36] the attainment of such happiness concerns intellectual virtue, which involves a journey through the various levels of cognition, employing the faculty of judgment along the way, solely for the purposes of a pragmatic proficiency for the good, in accordance with man's nature (fiṭrah); in view of this, practical virtue is exercised, whose sole purpose is to carry out the dictates of the faculty of judgment, and finally terminating at the knowledge of God. The realisation of true happiness depends on the Soul's ability to comprehend the immaterial nature of the Active

---

[34] Ibid., 119.
[35] Ibid., 123.
[36] Ibid.

Intellect. The fate of the Soul is also dependant upon this realisation. Al-Fārābī argues that unless the Soul is able to comprehend the immaterial nature of the Active Intellect, it "will appear in one material condition after another, either endlessly, if they are fated to be reincarnated in human form, or until such time as they have degenerated by degrees, to the bestial level, whereupon they will simply perish".[37] Clearly on this point, al-Fārābī's views were radically antithetical to the Quranic doctrine denying the transmigration of Souls.

Abū Zakariyyā Yaḥyā b. ʿAdī ibn Ḥamīd b. Zakariyyā al-Takrītī al-Manṭiqī (d. 363H/974CE), a Monophysite Christian, was a student of al-Fārābī and Abū Bishr Mattā ibn Yūnus. We need only mention that he was of the same opinion as the latter in terms of the separability of logic from grammar, perhaps for the same reasons stated earlier. With regard to his epistemology, logic was afforded the dual task of being a tool on the one hand, while on the other, a necessary prelude to the study of theology. Therefore, knowledge dependant on a correct and thorough appreciation of logic, constituted deliverance from error and hence, to Paradise. In terms of this knowledge, what may be known, and how it may be known, rested on perception. Perception is then viewed as the path to logic. Yet, perception is intrinsically fallible, hence, the same is also

---

[37] Al-Fārābī, *Al-Madīnah al-Faḍīlah* (Beirut, 1959). Quoted from *A History of Islamic Philosophy*, 127. See also, Richard Walzer, *Al-Farabi on the Perfect State: Abū Naṣr al-Fārābī's Mabādiʾ Ārāʾ ahl al-Madīna al-Faḍīla* (Oxford: Clarendon Press, 1985), 259-77.

logic.[38] This apparent antinomy however, did not seem in any way to prejudice his belief in Christian doctrine. Indeed, his pessimistic views on the fallibility of perception as the primary tool of the intellect only strengthened his conviction towards the doctrine of original sin.[39] Although he had been al-Fārābī's student, his reaction towards the *mutakallimūn*, and Islām in general, was hostile. He was a renowned theologian whose claim to posterity in Islamic thought is by virtue of his polemical arguments with Muslim theologians of the time.[40] Both Ibn Abī Usaybi'ah and Abū Ḥayyān al-Tawḥīdī make reference to Yaḥyā ibn 'Adī with caution in one respect, contending that the latter did not always fully grasp the more esoteric meanings contained in certain metaphysical doctrines while, in other respects, both reserve unsolicited praise for Yaḥyā ibn 'Adī.[41] In defence of an anti-Trinitarian polemic composed by al-Kindī, he wrote a rebuttal entitled *Tabyīn Ghalaṭ Abū Yūsuf Ya'qūb ibn Isḥāq al-Kindī fī Maqālatihā fī'l Radd 'alā'l Naṣārā*,[42] which then perhaps became part of a larger polemic for subsequent discussions between Muslim and Christian theologians. His explanation and defence of the Trinity was heavily influenced not only by the Christian attribution of 'blind' faith, but also by Aristotelian-Neoplatonic postulates with regard to the intellect.[43] In this

---

[38] *Al-Fārābī and his School*, 57.
[39] Ibid., 59.
[40] *A History of Islamic Philosophy*, 196.
[41] Ibid., 8.
[42] *Al-Fārābī and his School*, 10.
[43] Ibid., 61-62.

respect, his concept of intellect owed "nothing to the tenfold emanationist hierarchy of his master, al-Fārābī",[44] for clearly, his concept included a Trinitarian dimension. "In the period after Yaḥyā ibn 'Adī, Christian disciples tended to adhere to Christian scholars, and Muslim disciples gravitated towards Muslim scholars".[45] One possible exception to this rule was in the person of Abū Sulaymān Muḥammad b. Ṭāhir b. Bahrām al-Sijistānī al-Mantiqī (circa 300H/912CE-375H/985CE).[46]

Al-Sijistānī, philosopher, scientist and mathematician, bore the honorific title "philosopher of the Arabs".[47] The *Siwān al-Ḥikmah*, composed by him, is perhaps the oldest known source concerned with the history of Islamic and Greek philosophical traditions, and therefore, is probably the first to identify five philosophers as the embodiment of the *Ikhwān al-Safā'*.[48] Due to the fact that a large number of his works are not extant, what we do know about him and his philosophical tradition, may be gleaned through the al-Muqābasāt of his contemporary and companion Abū Ḥayyān al-Tawḥīdī.[49] Al-Sijistānī objected to the attempts by the

---

[44] Ibid., 63.

[45] *Humanism in the Renaissance of Islam*, 139-140.

[46] These dates are given by Kraemer. See *Humanism in the Renaissance of Islam*. Netton offers a slightly different estimation although he too quotes Kraemer as his source basing his estimation of dates on Kraemer's earlier work for his PhD thesis; see *Al-Fārābī and his School*, 11.

[47] *A History of Islamic Philosophy*, 68.

[48] Ibid., 164.

[49] *Al-Fārābī and his School*, 63. Unfortunately, such works were unavailable to us and therefore, we have had to rely upon the reports of Netton, Fakhry, and Kraemer.

Ikhwān al-Safā' to harmonise religion and philosophy. The former aims at seeking proximity to God, while the latter only serves to contemplate creation. The ultimate aim of philosophy according to al-Sijistānī, however, was knowledge. In this sense, both sought the arrival of certainty. Contemplation, on the one hand, led to the certainty of a creator. Both contemplation and the arrival of certain knowledge in the soul as a result, was a reflection of God's power, the recognition of which is also confirmed by religion. In this way, piety and submission to Him are fostered. Al-Sijistānī's doctrine of the soul and its relationship to the body preoccupied him. For him, the soul "is a simple substance, independent of body; hence immortal".[50] He observes that "it is difficult for man to know the soul, for he can only know the soul by means of his soul, and he is veiled from his soul by his soul".[51] What is interesting to note here is that according to Netton, al-Sijistānī, like his teacher before him, thought of the soul in terms of a 'tripartite' division. Netton concludes that both al-Sijistānī and Yahyā ibn 'Adī associated this tripartite division of the soul with the "Platonic doctrine of the tri-partition of the soul corresponding virtues".[52] In this regard, are we sure that Yahyā ibn 'Adī was solely influenced by the

---

[50] *Philosophy in the Renaissance of Islam*, 139. Since the body is compound, it is corruptible; hence finite. The soul on the other hand is simple and therefore, incorruptible. That which is corrupti-ble cannot be part of a unity which is incorruptible, therefore the soul must be separate from the body.

[51] Ibid., 226. See also *Al-Fārābī and his School*, 65.

[52] *Al-Fārābī and his School*, 64.

Platonic doctrine concerning the tripartition of the soul, or could Christian doctrine also have had an influence on his doctrine? We have shown in Chapter Four, with regard to our general framework of the Western worldview that, historically, the Christian church adopted Aristotelian Neo-Platonic postulates in order to legitimise their religion. If this is true, we may also conclude that his tripartite division of the soul was duly influenced by Christian dogma. But to what extent did his beliefs influence al-Sijistānī? Was al-Sijistānī also convinced of the legitimacy of the tripartite division as interpreted by Yahyā ibn 'Adī in the religious sense? Netton does not appear to be making such an implication, instead he says that al-Sijistānī was "also familiar with an Aristotelian tripartite division of the soul into the vegetative (*al-nāmiyyah*), animal (*al-ḥayawāniyyah*) and the rational (*al-nāṭiqah*)".[53] This has nothing to do with a tripartition of the soul's corresponding virtues, because virtue, understood in Islām, implies that one must have knowledge. This knowledge is not the kind of knowledge found in either the vegetative or the animal soul. Indeed, it is the kind of knowledge that presumes reason, will and intent; therefore, virtues are particular to the rational soul of man. In order to correctly discern al-Sijistānī's understanding of the soul, reference must be made in connection with his understanding of knowledge.

In reference to knowledge, al-Sijistānī proposes that the soul of man has a dual nature; bestial (*al-nafs al-*

---

[53] Ibid.

shahwiyyah) and rational (*al-nafs al-'āqilah*).[54] In this context, he does not construct a tripartite division of the soul as alleged by Netton. Here, it is clear that virtue cannot belong to the animal soul, for it does not possess the power of intellectual discernment, the power to interpret the meaning of reality and truth; nor does it aspire to seek ultimate happiness. The animal soul, as the name suggests, is concerned only with satisfying its appetitive desires. For it, happiness is momentary and fleeting. Everything concerned with the animal soul is directed to the temporality of this world. Its task is simply to preserve the body, and is, therefore, subordinate to the rational soul. Hence, it is unclear what is meant by Netton. Does al-Sijistānī construct a tripartite division of the soul in terms of knowledge? Unfortunately, al-Sijistānī does not show if he has developed a hierarchy in terms of knowledge. We may only speculate that he did in fact develop such a hierarchy because according to him, knowledge belongs to the rational soul, and that knowledge is "the fruit or the yield of the intellect".[55] Al-Sijistānī's division of the intellect closely resembles the sixfold division envisaged by al-Fārābī. Therefore, by virtue of this fact, there must also be a hierarchy in terms of knowledge. Once again however, it is not clear if this hierarchy is tripartite.

Although there may be some truth to Netton's argument in terms of the fact that al-Sijistānī was duly influenced by Greek texts, we do not agree with the implication that those

---

[54] Ibid., 68.
[55] Ibid., 69.

very texts were the fundamental basis for the development of his system.[56] We are convinced that al-Sijistānī could not have held the opinion of Yahyā ibn 'Adī with reference to the tripartite division of the soul if, in fact, it was interpreted by the latter in the Christian dogmatic sense. We know this by virtue of his doctrine concerning the intellect which has authority over soul. "The intellect (al-'aql)", according to al-Sijistānī, "is the Caliph of God. It is the recipient of the pure emanation (al-fayḍ al-khāliṣ) which has neither blemish nor impurity. If one said that intellect were absolute light (nūr fī'l ghāya), one would not be far wrong".[57] The analogy with

---

[56] This appears to be a common trend with the Orientalists, namely to deny originality to Islamic theoretical sciences. Every theory advanced by Muslims sciences, it is argued, has its roots in Aristotelianism, Platonism, Neoplatonism, was borrowed from the Plotinian school, or is ascribed to Philloponus (Yahyā al-Naḥwī). A case in point, Nicholas Rescher, in the introduction to *Studies in the History of Arabic Logic* (Pittsburgh: University of Pittsburg Press, 1963), 13, states that "Arabic logic, *like the rest of medieval Arabic science and philosophy is entirely Western*" (Italics are my own to show emphasis). We have mentioned that this denies originality to Muslim sciences. We have further mentioned with regard to the worldview of Islām and of the ability of Islām to borrow from other cultures. In doing so however, the fundamental elements of the resultant sciences in Islām did not, as a consequence, adopt those same foundations, in this case Greek fundamental postulates. There was no need for Muslim scientists to do so because the fundamental elements which formed the basis of these sciences were already described by the worldview of Islām. Simply because Western sciences did not possess a legitimate worldview, let alone a scientific tradition of their own without the influence of Greek thought, does not presume the same to be true of Muslim scientific traditions.

[57] Ibid., 66.

reference to emanation, according to Netton, follows the "Neoplatonic dimension of al-Sijistānī's thought".[58] But what about the reference to light? We have previously mentioned that the aim of philosophy is contemplation, and this contemplation results in the arrival of certitude in the soul concerning God and is confirmed by religion. Since the intellect has authority over the soul, clearly then, this light would convey certitude to the soul through direct perception. The Qur'ān often uses the analogy of light as a clear manifestation to mean convincing proof concerning God.[59] Therefore, in light of al-Sijistānī's interpretation concerning the ultimate aim of philosophy, it becomes clear that his analogy of light does not follow an interpretation through the sieve of Greek Neoplatonic thought; rather it follows one born from an interpretation of Quranic doctrine.

Although al-Sijistānī was schooled in the Fārābian tradition, his opinions concerning philosophy differed with regard to prophecy and its relation to philosophy. Al-Fārābī taught that prophetic truth was actually the highest form of philosophy, attained by virtue of a noetic synergy between the intellects of the prophets and the Active Intellect. In essence, prophets are philosophers of a superior rank. Al-Sijistānī did not agree with this conception, adopting instead an approach to prophecy which was akin to al-Kindī's conception. Prophecy, he maintained, is superior in rank to philosophy. The kind of knowledge attained by prophets is divine, therefore it is transcendental, acquired directly with-

---

[58] Ibid.
[59] 4/al-Nisā', 174-175.

out the medium of human limitation. Knowledge acquired through philosophical means is speculative, and thus, limited. Indeed, that which is limited by reason cannot penetrate the realm of transcendental knowledge.[60]

Ibn Sīnā's comprehension of God as Absolute Necessary Being, and the created order of existents that are in themselves only possible, would later contribute to an understanding of creation in the West. According to Ibn Sīnā:

"When some thing through its own essence is continuously a cause for the existence of some other thing, it is a cause for it continuously exists as long as its essence continues existing. If it [the cause] exists continuously, then that which is caused exists continuously. Thus, what is like this [cause] is among the highest causes, for it prevents the non-existence of something, and is that which gives perfect existence to something. This is the meaning of that which is called 'creation' [ibda'] by the philosophers, namely, the bringing into existence of something after absolute non-existence. For it belongs to that which is caused, in itself, that it does not exist [laysa], while it belongs to it from its cause that it does exist [aysa]. That which belongs to something in itself is prior, according to the mind, in essence, not in time to that which comes from another. Thus, everything which is caused is existing after non-existing by a posteriority in terms of essence. ... If [an effect's] existence comes after absolute non-existence, its emanation from the cause in this way is called ibda' ("absolute origination").

---

[60] See *Philosophy in the Renaissance of Islam*, 242.

This is the most excellent form of the bestowal of existence, for (in this case) non-existence has simply been prevented and existence has been given the sway *ab initio*."[61]

Ibn Sīnā goes on to note the distinction between the ways in which metaphysicians and natural philosophers discuss causality with respect to creation:

"... the metaphysicians do not intend by the agent the principle of movement only, as do the natural philosophers, but also the principle of existence and that which bestows existence, such as the creator of the world."[62]

Ibn Sīnā's distinction between essence and existence is part of his intellectual contribution aimed at comprehending the intelligible natures of things. His sympathy for an emanationist scheme, according to which all existents effuse from a primal source of Being, betrays his ontological priority. His discussion with regard to necessary and possible existent forms the crux of his distinction between essence and existence. In his system, essence is something prior and to which existence occurs as an accident.[63] 'Real existence'

---

[61] Ibn Sīnā, *al-Shifā': al-Ilahiyyāt*, vII. 266, quoted in Barry Kogan, *Averroes and the Metaphysics of Causation* (Binghamton: State University of New York Press, 1985), 276, n. 58.

[62] Ibid., vI., 1, quoted in A. Hyman and J. Walsh (ed.), *Philosophy in the Middle Ages*, 2nd edition (Hackett, 1983), 248.

[63] David Burrell, "Aquinas and Islamic and Jewish Thinkers", in Norman Kretzmann and Eleonore Stump (eds.) *The Cambridge*

then emerges as something superadded to the contingent being prior to which was originally an essence or possibility in God's mind. Goodman observes:

"The key to Ibn Sina's synthesis of the metaphysics of contingency with the metaphysics of necessity lies in the simple phrase: *considered in itself*. Considered in itself, each effect is radically contingent. It does not contain the conditions of its own existence; and, considered in itself, it need not exist. Its causes give it being. It is by abstracting from its causes that we can regard even the world as a whole as radically contingent. But considered in relation to its causes, not as something that in the abstract might not have existed, but as something concretely given before us, with a determinate character, the same conditionedness that required us to admit its contingency requires us to admit its necessity. Considered in relation to its causes, this object must exist, in the very Aristotelian sense that it does exist, and must have the nature that it has in that its causes gave it that nature. A thing might *have been* other than as it is, it might yet be other than it is, but it cannot *now* be other than it is."[64]

For Ibn Sīnā, the world is conceived as being both eternal and necessary, not something subject to His act of creating by free will. In doing so, he sought to assert

---

Companion to Aquinas (Cambridge: Cambridge University Press, 1993), 69.
[64] Goodman, *Avicenna* (London: Routledge, 1992), 66-67.

contingency of the created order.[65] The world proceeds from God by necessity and is eternal; however, it is only possible in itself and requires a cause in order to exist. On the other hand, God is Necessary in Himself and, hence, is not in need of a cause. Aristotle explains in the *Posterior Analytics* that knowledge, truly deserving of the name science, is the knowledge of a necessary nexus between cause and effect.[66] That existence which is not necessary in itself, but necessary by something other than itself, is known as contingent existence which, in Ibn Sīnā's view, did not contravene the idea of natural necessity. In relation to God then, finite existents, while contingent in themselves, are necessary with reference to their causes, for without this necessary nexus, the world of created things would remain unintelligible. However, an admission that the world is one created by God was undeniable, for if the opposite were assumed, namely that the world was a product of necessity, then a further assumption with regard to its self sufficiency must be postulated, and this is impossible. The possibility of a necessary world must needs an assumption that it issues from a primal source whose being is eternal (*qadīm*). Hence, the theory of emanation appeared to justify the arguments pertaining to the absolute origin of the world since it addressed both problems of necessity and contingency.

Ibn Sīnā held that creation was an ontological problem, having admitted that the theory of emanation is only possi-

---

[65] Ibid., 63.

[66] Jonathan Barnes (ed.), *The Complete Works of Aristotle* (Princeton: Princeton University Press, 1995), v. 1, 114-166.

ble within the framework of an eternal universe. What is meant by an ontological problem is one where the order of being has no reference to temporality. In addition, the theory of emanation denied God a free will. In essence, Ibn Sīnā much like al-Fārābī, opposed the idea of creation, preferring instead an emanationist conception. It was precisely this irreconcilable conception held by Ibn Sīnā that led to the attack on his philosophy by Hujjat al-Islām Abū Ḥāmid Muḥammad b. Muḥammad b. Muḥammad al-Ghazzālī al-Ṭūsī (450-505H/1058-1111CE). All the while, the persistent political and economic crises, compounded by the empty monotony of the anti-scholastic, anti-intellectual Hanbalite orthodoxy, caused the religious malaise all too eager to stress the law (*sharī'ah*) and reduce everything to that which is permitted (*halāl*), and that which is forbidden (*harām*). The time was now set for 'the man'.

"With the time came the man"; this is how Duncan Black MacDonald, in his now famous *Development of Muslim Theology, Jurisprudence and Constitutional Theory*, introduces al-Ghazzālī. The time al-Ghazzālī lived was a time of political turmoil and agitation; the 'Abbāsid cali- phate was in a state of abasement in danger of losing Baghdad, Spain was in a state of chaotic revolt, and the different political alliances and religious sectarianism had limited all intellectual inquiry to the narrow confines of the law. It was also during this time that the Bāṭinite peril was on the upsurge. The greatest effects from the influence of Persian philosophy were manifest in extremist Shi'ite beliefs. This was an age "characterised by a kind of intemperateness in thought and an unruliness in imagination which led to an extraordinary confusion and a curious concern with religions and sects and movements, with each tongue and pen going its own way".[67]

Al-Ghazzālī was an extraordinary polymathic genius whose authoritative grasp of knowledge did not limit his capacity to that of jurist, theologian, philosopher and mystic. Indeed, it was he who answered the call of Islām to defend against what were considered to be attacks aimed at the very core of the fundamental elements of the religion.

Even in his youth, al-Ghazzālī was not alien to prejudice and envy. Indeed, the Imām al-Ḥaramayn was one such person who did not hold a sincere private regard for him simply because al-Ghazzālī was one whose intellectual capacity superceded his own. There he quenched his thirst for knowledge with other luminaries whose reputations, much like al-Ghazzālī's would, had preceded them. But he was like no other, none could match his authoritative grasp of knowledge in both the sciences and the humanities. After having mastered the science of 'foundations' (*'ilm al-Uṣūl*), he composed several books and subsequently refurbished the Shāfi'ite school of jurisprudence. This only led to more calumniation from his detractors and the opposition. He was the brunt of much slander and vilification, but remained unaffected by it. The writing of the *al-Munqidh min al-Ḍalāl* (Deliverance from Error) was written precisely because he had grown weary of the corruption, in terms of knowledge, and hastened to clarify the many misconceptions.

---

[67] R.J. McCarthy, *Freedom and Fulfilment* (Boston: Twayne Publishers, 1980), xii.

Attempts to suppress his genius however, would not escape the attentions of the Master, Nizām al-Mulk. The latter had taken an interest in al-Ghazzālī by virtue of his excellence in disputation and the fact that he was the inspiration of the men of learning, the intentions of the religious scholars and the pride of the men of letters. After nearly ten years in isolation as part of his "battle against self and to regulate his character and to improve his qualities and to rectify his lifestyle",[68] he was called to the Nizāmiyyah[69] where his career began once again to flourish. Later, when asked why he had decided to forsake his 'search' and accept Nizām al-Mulk's invitation he replied, "According to my religion I could not conceivably hold back from the summons and the utility of benefiting the seekers of [knowledge]. It was indeed imperative for me to disclose the truth and to speak of it and to call to it".[70] Needless to say, al-Ghazzālī was emulating the famous hadīth, "When someone is asked about knowledge, and he hides it, on the day of judgment (qiyāmah) he will be thrown to hellfire".[71]

In his monumental work, Tahāfut al-Falāsifah (the Incoherence of the Philosophers), which represents a refutation of philosophy in general, he outlined twenty points of contention with the philosophers; three of which were deemed irreligious, for he says:

---

[68] Ibid., xvi.
[69] The school established by Nizām al-Mulk which also bears his name.
[70] Freedom and Fulfilment, op. cit., xix.
[71] See Ibn Mājah, Sunan Abū Dāūd, 24:1.

"To brand the philosophers with infidelity is inevitable, so far as three problems are concerned-namely (1) the problem of the eternity of the world, where they maintained that all the substances are eternal. (2) their assertion that Divine knowledge does not encompass individual objects (3) their denial of the resurrection of bodies. All these three theories are in violent opposition to Islām. To believe in them is to accuse the prophets of falsehood, and to consider their teachings as a hypocritical misrepresentation designed to appeal to the masses. And this is blatant blasphemy to which no Muslim sect would subscribe."[72]

In his *al-Munqidh min al-Ḍalāl*, al-Ghazzālī reiterates his conviction with regard to the infidelity of the philosophers, saying:

"In the three questions ... they [the philosophers] were opposed to [the belief] of all Muslims, viz. in their affirming (1) that men's bodies will not be assembled on the Last Day, but only disembodied spirits will be rewarded and punished, and the rewards and punishments will be spiritual, not corporeal ... they falsely denied the corporeal rewards and punishments and blasphemed the revealed Law in their stated views. (2) The second question is their declaration: 'God Most High knows universals, but not particulars'. This also is out-and-out unbelief ... (3) The third question is their maintaining the eternity of the world, past and

---

[72] Sabih Ahmad Kamali, *Al-Ghazali's Tahafut al-Falasifah* (Lahore: Pakistan Philosophical Congress, 1963), 249.

future. No Muslim has ever professed any of their views on these questions."[73]

Al-Ghazzālī regarded Ibn Sīnā's adherence to the idea of an eternal world, as opposed to that of creation, to be the antithesis of the sacrosanct tenets of Islām. An eternal world, he proposed, is completely independent of God's will since it is by definition self sufficient. In addition, God cannot be Necessary Agent, because an agent, by definition, requires will, whereas Necessary, by definition, does not. Therefore, the two, Necessary and Agent, are in fact a contradiction, and this is impossible in reference to God. Similarly, al-Ghazzālī professes that, even on philosophical grounds, all the arguments advanced for an eternal world fall short and are, therefore, devoid of meaning. We have shown that Ibn Sīnā believed the world to be eternal and yet simultaneously created, yet not posterior to God in time but rather co-existing with God. In reply, al-Ghazzālī argues that what is meant by a created world is one that has an absolute temporal beginning. Understood in this context, it is not possible for God and time to be co-existent, for if time had an absolute beginning, then this would, by implication, mean that God also has an absolute beginning, and this is absurd. More importantly, the world cannot be both eternal and created, as argued by Ibn Sīnā, because that which is created implies an absolute beginning whereas that which is eternal does not. Therefore, this too is absurd.

---

[73] Al-Ghazzālī, *al-Munqidh min al-Dalāl*. Quoted from Lenn E. Goodman, *An Introduction to Medieval Islamic Philosophy*, 20-21.

Al-Ghazzālī's greatest work, his magnum opus, was undoubtedly his *Iḥyā' 'Ulūm al-Dīn*, which he composed after the death of his patron, Niẓām al-Mulk. The latter had been assassinated by a zealous fanatic allied to Hassan al-Sabāḥ, the Bāṭinite despot. Thereafter, one of al-Ghazzālī's primary concerns was to address the threat posed to Islām by Bāṭinism. The assassination of his patron then became his motive for writing the aforementioned book. The *Iḥyā'* consists of four 'quarters' (*aqsām*), each comprising ten 'books' (*kitāb*).

The first two books of the first quarter comprise the definition of knowledge and the foundations of orthodox belief; the rest consider the ritual acts of worship as prescribed by the five pillars of Islām. On knowledge, al-Ghazzālī's classification denotes that there are two kinds of knowledge; necessary (*wājib*), and beneficial (*nāfi'*), the former referring to the Quranic sciences, the latter to the other branches of the sciences from which one may derive benefit. It cannot escape the attention of the student of learning that every argument, every elucidation, every proof put forth by al-Ghazzālī, appealed to reason in conformity with revelation. Reason, according to him, "is the source of science, its beginning and its basis; science is to reason like fruit are to trees and light is to the sun and sight is to the eye".[74] Reason was not considered prior to revelation but was used as a tool, as a method to deduce from the Qur'ān, the 'keys' to all of the sciences. In considering the sciences deemed by him to be beneficial, he warns the novice against

---

[74] Al-Ghazzālī, *Iḥyā' 'Ulūm al-Dīn* (Beirut: Dār al-Kutub al-'Ilmiyyah, 1986), v. 1, 99.

advancing further in search of the theoretical foundations without first having a firm grasp of the conceptual philosophical interdependencies between them.[75] Indeed the *Iḥyā'* dealt a 'death blow' to the encroachment of fanaticism and extremism seeking to establish a foothold, and remains a reference manual for those seeking to revive the intellectual splendour of Muslim intellectualism.

---

[75] Ibid., 26-55.

SIX

'ISLAM HADHARI' EXPLAINED

EARLIER WE HAVE made mention of the fact that the government's current intentions, with regard to the ideological milieu, is to vigorously promote what is referred to as a 'mental revolution'. The only possible assumption, with regard to the term 'mental', is that it refers to the mind, in which case, we may further conclude that what is intended by the government, is to encourage a rational and dynamic thinking which is crucial to understanding. According to the Prime Minister, it is "imperative for Muslims to unshackle our minds and, further, to acquire and master the sciences and technology in order to stay relevant in the modern world".[1] In addition, "the men of understanding the Qur'ān refers to, are people of reason, of science, of philosophy and of technology".[2] We take great interest in the following

---

[1] See the article "Muslim world needs a meeting of minds" published in the *New Straits Times*, Tuesday, the 5th of October 2004.
[2] Ibid.

quotation uttered by the Prime Minister during the recent UMNO General Assembly. According to him, "UMNO's strength has been proven to be predicated on a more astute approach, based on reason and rationale. Such an approach must be continued and acculturated within UMNO, consistent with the Quranic injunction", which he goes on to quote:

> "Invite (all) to the way of thy Lord with wisdom and beautiful preaching; and argue with them in ways that are best and most gracious; for thy Lord knoweth best, who have strayed from his path, and who receive guidance."[3]

The term used in the Qur'ān to mean wisdom is *hikmah*. The meanings of 'wisdom', 'beautiful preaching' and 'argue with them in ways that are best' are generally understood and accepted among Muslim logicians to denote the science of logic.

Therefore, in order to fulfil the prerequisite requirements of reason, one needs to first familiarise oneself with logic.

The reason it is incumbent to do so, is because there are two ways that knowledge, that is to say the perception of things which is expressed through the arrival of the form of a thing in the mind, together with the meaning of those produced forms, is acquired. The first is through conception (*tasawwur*) void of judgment, while the other is declarative

---

[3] 16/al-Nahl, 125. Translation of the verse is from Abdullah Yusuf Ali, *The Meaning of the Holy Qur'ān* (Brentwood, Maryland: Amana Corporation, 1991).

(*tasdīq*), which is acquired through the combination of both conception and judgment. Some knowledge derived from each of the two, are self-evident (*badīhī*), while some others are theoretical (*nazarī*), which are derived from the self-evident through reflection. Reflection is not precise without employing the rules of logic. Logic (*al-Mantiq*), therefore, is the science where notions of conceptive and declarative knowledge are inquired into, that is to say how this knowledge is arranged so that it leads to unknown conceptions and declarations. The benefit of logic is in order to know how to think correctly. In other words, it is the correct arrangement of issues that are known in order to arrive at the unknown, and to know its corruption.

The science of logic is to be considered the most pure owing to the fact that it is the most formal. Logic considered in itself, is a science, but when it is applied to the study of philosophy, it is a tool employed by the theoretical sciences in order that correct conclusions may be reached based on sound proofs and supported by valid arguments which conform to the rules of logic. And so, just as our knowledge of things begins with the simplest elements which are understood by means of simple concepts, logic begins with conceptions (*tasawwur*). These conceptions are based primarily on perception. They are then given intelligible meaning when the intellect derives meaning from what is perceived. In order to do so, it has to make judgments; these are acquired through assent (*tasdīq*). By virtue of assent, the mind is able to understand what it perceives. Some judgments are made intuitively without the medium of the external senses.

We may propose that Muslim logicians consider logic as a science which analyses the elements of knowledge. This approach assumes that in analysing the elements of knowledge, we acquire the basic means to knowledge. This basic means to knowledge therefore, constitutes the first major division of logic, called *taṣawwurāt*, the principles by which the acquisition of knowledge of the fundamental elements are still required. By virtue of this, we then embark upon combining these elements meaningfully, logically, in other words consistently and systematically, in order to expand the scope of our knowledge. This constitutes the second division of logic, called *taṣdīqāt*. That is why, according to Muslim logicians, knowledge is divided into two kinds:

1. Conceptions or mental perceptions (*taṣawwurāt*), which is the kind of knowledge that does not adjudicate; it merely apprehends the image of existent forms in the mind. It is this apprehended image that we call 'concept'. Some conceptions are grasped intuitively (*badīhī*), or *a priori*, while others are deduced or theoretical (*naẓarī*). Using logical reasoning as a tool, deductive concepts may be derived from, or founded upon intuitive, or *a priori* concepts.
2. Judgments (*taṣdīqāt*),[4] which is the kind of knowledge that utilises the apprehended images (concepts), and makes an assertion that something is true. This assertion

---

[4] Judgment (*taṣdīq*), or Assent, or Declaration is the verbal noun derived from *ṣādiq* which means to be true, and therefore *taṣdīq* is an assertion that something is true. Often it is used for phrases that are known to be true, for example: "The world is temporal".

is an affirmation of the correspondence between the concept and the thing represented by it. Like conceptions, some declarations are grasped intuitively (*badīhī*), or *a priori*, while others are deduced, or theoretical (*naẓarī*). Similarly, using logical reasoning as a tool, deductive concepts may be derived from intuitive, or *a priori* concepts.

It is apparent then, that conception precedes declaration, given that every declaration must first contain the conception or the assertion of the subject, following which, a judgment that the relation between subject and predicate is or is not taking place; however, while every declaration presupposes conception, the converse is not true. The subjects of a science are those that have been appointed or that have been designated, and which are inquired into, either essentially, or partially. The logician inquires into these two kinds of knowledge (i.e. *taṣawwur* and *taṣdīq*), so far as it leads to the unknown contained within them, and so far as it leads to other conceptions and declarations. The conceptions which lead to other conceptions are the five universals; that is to say genus (*jins*), species (*naw'*), general accident (*'araḍ*), differentia (*faṣl*) and property (*khāṣṣah*).

Muslim logicians, therefore, consider concepts to be the most simple and fundamental elements of our knowledge. Just as 'words' are the most primary elements of our language, because thought and language are reflexive, in the same way, our thought has concepts as its simple elements. How then do concepts achieve meaning? This is achieved by way of denotation (*al-dalālah*), which refers to something's

129

being in such a way that its knowledge requires the knowledge or conjecture of something else; or, the conjecture of which requires the conjecture of that thing. It becomes clear from this definition that the way to know what something is, is through a phrase defining or explaining what that something is. The explanatory phrase is a denotative means used to arrive at unknown conceptions from known conceptions. It is also called the definer or *definiens* (*al-mu'arrif*), because it points to its true nature.

It is the explanatory phrase which concerns us here, because as we have mentioned at the onset, the phrase 'Islam hadhari' is just that. And therefore, knowledge concerning the rudiments of the explanatory phrase equips the reader with an understanding of how to proceed. There are two kinds of explanatory phrase; definition (*hadd*) and description (*rasm*).

It is not permissible to define a thing by its quiddity because it would assume that the definition would be known prior to the thing defined, which would mean that the thing defined would be known before itself. A thing must not be defined by something more general than the thing to be defined, or its definition would fall short of the truth. Similarly, a thing must not be defined by something more peculiar than the thing to be defined, or it will remain obscure.[5] The explanatory phrase is an expression leading to

---

[5] I have extracted a general summation of the ways of defining from A. Sprenger's translation of the *Risālah Shamsiyyah fī 'Ilm al-Mantiq* by Mawlāna Najm al-Dīn Kātibī Qazwinī, contained in the "First Appendix to the Dictionary of the Technical Terms Used in the Sciences of the Mussalmans, Containing the Logic of the

definition. There are two kinds of definition and two kinds of description. Definition is a construction in which the genus is indicated along with its difference. In order to capture the essence of the thing defined with respect to all other things, the definition has to indicate all the differences pertaining to it. Complete definition (*ḥadd tāmm*) is a definition that incorporates the proximate genus and the proximate difference of the thing to be defined.[6] Incomplete definition (*ḥadd nāqiṣ*) is a definition that incorporates the proximate difference and the remote genus of the thing to be defined.[7]

Description is also a construction in which the genus is indicated, however, contrary to definition, a description includes property, which is part of the essence, and is true for all realities contained within the species. A complete description (*rasm tāmm*), literally taken to mean a representation or illustration, is a description that incorporates property and the proximate genus. In an incomplete description (*rasm nāqiṣ*), the proximate genus is excluded,

---

Arabians in the Original Arabic, with an English Translation". It should be further noted that care should be observed not to define a thing that is coextensive with the thing defined, for example, defining 'motion' as being 'not at rest'; or, defining 'even' as being 'not odd'.

[6] For example, 'animal' and 'rational' with regard to 'man'. By incorporating both the proximate genus, 'animal', and the proximate difference, 'rational', a complete definition of 'man' as 'rational animal' is achieved.

[7] For example, 'rational' and 'being' with regard to 'man'. By incorporating the proximate difference, 'rational', and the remote genus, 'being', an incomplete definition of 'man' as 'rational being' is achieved.

and it may include property alone,[8] property and remote genus,[9] property, remote genus and general accident,[10] and property and difference.

Having said that, let us now direct our attention to the phrase 'Islam hadhari'. We intend to briefly discuss the problems concerned with its definition from two aspects. The first will be from the point of view of reason, followed by a discussion from the etymological aspect. From the logical aspect of reason, the purpose of definition is to capture the essence of the thing defined, in other words, the meaning of the thing defined must lead to intelligible meaning. Therefore, in terms of the phrase 'Islam hadhari', three questions must be answered: Is the phrase receptive of a definition? If it is not receptive of a definition, then is it receptive of description? If the answers to both questions are in the affirmative, then does its definition or description lead to intelligible meaning?

We have said that definition is a construction in which the genus is indicated along with its difference. Hence, in order to define the aforementioned phrase, the genus would be indicated by the term 'Islam', while its difference would be indicated by the term 'hadhari'. But we have said earlier that Islām is perfect. By virtue of the fact that it is perfect, it is *not* receptive of classification into genus, species or differentia. Therefore, to say that the phrase is receptive of definition is absurd.

---

[8] For example, 'writing' in reference to 'man'.
[9] For example, 'writing body' in reference to 'man'.
[10] For example, 'writing black haired body' in reference to 'man'.

In the same token, if we were to examine the phrase 'Islam hadhari', the term 'Islam' denotes the name of the religion and is therefore, a noun (*ism*). In addition, the term 'hadhari', denotes the adjective (*sifah*) used to describe the noun. This further assumes that there is difference. But we have said that Islām is *not* receptive of differentia, and therefore, to say that the phrase is receptive of definition in this manner is also absurd.

So is it possible to describe the phrase 'Islam hadhari'? We have said that description, is a construction in which the genus is indicated, which includes property, which is part of the essence, and is true for all realities contained within the species. We have previously argued that Islām is not receptive of classification into genus, species or differentia. Having said that, one may only conclude that it is *not* possible to describe the phrase in a manner which will lead to intelligible meaning.

We have also said that concepts are given intelligible meaning when the intellect derives meaning from what is perceived. In order to do so, the thing perceived has to be defined. Since we have shown that the aforementioned phrase is neither receptive of a definition nor description, it cannot convey intelligible meaning. We must conclude therefore, that the phrase 'Islam hadhari' is *not* a concept.

If one were to examine the aforementioned phrase from the etymological aspect, then it is incumbent to examine the etymological roots of the terms. For the purpose of this book, we will not be examining the etymology of the term 'Islām' because there are already works dealing on the aforementioned subject matter, and therefore, we do not assume to be the authority on this subject.[11] Consequently, we will be analysing the term 'hadhari'.

To begin with, there appears to be a certain confusion in terms of the correct spelling of the term. Traditionally, words derived from, or having roots in the Arabic language, are transliterated into the English language according to an internationally recognised standard. We assume that the current understanding of the term 'hadhari' is a transliteration of the modern Arabic term derived from the root Ḥa Ḍa Ra, in other words, the sixth, fifteenth, and tenth letters of the Arabic alphabet. If our assumption is correct, then its subsequent transliteration 'hadhari' in incorrect. The letters 'dh' in 'hadhari' indicate the ninth letter of the alphabet, in which case its meaning also changes. But it has been understood to mean 'civilisational',[12] and therefore the correct transliteration should read *hadārī* with the long vowel on the letter 'a' and 'i', and with the omission of the second letter 'h'. If it were to be transliterated as *ḥadhāri*, then it would be understood to mean 'to beware', or 'to be cautious'. Clearly the latter meaning is not what is intended. Some may argue that the spelling of the transliterated word is done

---

[11] The works we refer to are most notably the works of Syed Muhammad Naquib al-Attas, principally his monograph, *Islam: The Concept of Religion and the Foundation of Ethics and Morality* (Kuala Lumpur: Dewan Bahasa dan Pustaka, 1992). This published monograph also constitutes the first chapter in his *Prolegomena*.

[12] We are referring to the way it has been understood according to the Minister in the Prime Minister's Department (Religious Affairs) following his interview on the subject published in the *New Sunday Times*, 1st August 2004.

according to the local vernacular, in which case we will answer, that if that were true, then there is no need for 'hadhari' to be spelled with a 'dh' as the 'h' is silent. If the pervading opinion is that it is not important to transliterate terms correctly, then we intend to show that this is truly the opinion of the minority. Supposing one were to assume that the second letter 'h' in 'hadhari' is ignored, and that the term *haḍari* is presumed accurate. The Arabic term *al-hadar* is used as a collective reference designating those living in cities, as opposed to the term *al-badw*, the collective reference designating those living nomadically. Consequently, an individual belonging to the former group is referred to as *haḍarī*. If the term 'hadhari' in the phrase 'Islam hadhari' refers the kind of Islām practised by one living in the city, it assumes that there is another kind of Islām practised by those not living in cities. This is absurd. But we have already mentioned the fact that the term 'hadhari' has been understood to mean 'civilisational', therefore, the correct transliteration of the term should read *hadārī*.

We have mentioned earlier that the term *haḍārī* is a modern Arabic term understood to mean 'civilisational' in the English language. However, this understanding of the term is unacceptable to Islām. This is by virtue of the fact that we have already mentioned in the previous chapters, that unlike Western civilisations, it is the worldview of Islām that determines and gives rise to culture, and consequently civilisation. And therefore, the Islamic civilisation is not one where the foundations for its worldview are deeply rooted in the rise of the sciences, whose premises are based solely on an ostensive preoccupation with the phenomenal world, nor does it suffer the vicissitudes determined by ideology, or described by historical periodisation. One may only conclude that this modern term has been offered in apology for the backwardness suffered by the Muslims of today. Although the Prime Minister himself has used the phrase 'civilisational Islam' to describe the approach known as 'Islam hadhari',[13] he does not mean civilisational in the manner we have described above. What the Prime Minister endorses is best reflected by the term *tamaddun*, one of the derivations from the term *dīn*, "meaning civilisation and refinement in social culture".[14] This understanding would consequently lead to intelligible meaning. Some may argue, why not use the phrase 'Islam madani' instead? We will answer that our arguments with reference to 'Islam hadhari' also apply. Furthermore, if one were possessed of a profound grasp of Islām, one will discover that it is erroneous to predicate such of Islām. So what does the Prime Minister mean when he advocates this approach referred to as 'Islam hadhari'?

In order to answer this question, an examination of what the Prime Minister intends is pertinent. In other words, what is the ultimate purpose (*maqṣūd*) of such an approach? He has said that the purpose of this approach is to:

"Enhance the quality of life. It aims to achieve this via the mastery of knowledge and the development

---

[13] See the article "Muslim world needs a meeting of minds", published in the *New Straits Times*, Tuesday, the 5th of October 2004.
[14] *Prolegomena*, 44.

of the individual and the nation; the implementation of a dynamic economic, trading and financial system; an integrated and balanced development that creates a knowledgeable and pious people who hold to noble values and are honest, trustworthy, and prepared to take on global challenges".[15]

He goes on to say that this approach, "is not a new religion. It is not a new teaching nor is it a new denomination (*madhhab*). It is an effort to bring the ummah back to basics, back to the fundamentals, as prescribed in the Qur'ān and the ḥadith that form the foundation of Islamic civilisation".[16] What does the approach aim to achieve? The Prime Minister enumerates ten principles;[17]

   i.   Faith and piety in Allāh;

   ii.   A just and trustworthy government;

   iii.   A free and independent people;

   iv.   A mastery of knowledge;

   v.   A balanced and comprehensive economic development;

   vi.   A good quality of life;

   vii.   Protection of the rights of minority groups and women;

   viii. Cultural and moral integrity;

   ix.   Safeguarding the environment; and

   x.   Strong defences

---

[15] See the Prime Minister's keynote address delivered at the UMNO General Assembly on the 23rd of September 2004 in Kuala Lumpur.

[16] Ibid.

[17] Ibid.

The Prime Minister believes this approach to be:

"Complete and comprehensive, with an emphasis on the development of the economy and civilisation, capable of building Malay competitiveness. The glorious heritage of Islamic civilisation in all aspects must be used as a reference and become the source of inspiration for the Malay race to prosper."[18]

But in order for the Malays to achieve prosperity, be it in terms of material wealth or in terms of spiritual happiness, they are required to change and rid themselves of those bestial characteristics detrimental to their own well being. We have already enumerated those characteristics deemed vile and requiring of change in Chapter Three. In order to convince the Malays that change is needed requires "action that is encompassing, drastic and systematic, regardless of sector or partisan loyalty. It requires the Malays to change their conceptions with regard to the world around them".[19] In light of this, any ideology which does not lead to intelligible meaning, or that leads to confusion and is antithetical to the worldview of Islām, "must be rejected".[20] What is most apparent is the fact that the Prime Minister emphasises that this change requires great effort (*ijtihād*) and great struggle (*jihād*). One must not be mislead along the path of confusion into thinking that the terms *ijtihād* and *jihād*, uttered by the Prime Minister in his keynote address during the UMNO

---

[18] Ibid.
[19] Ibid.
[20] Ibid.

General Assembly on the 23rd of September 2004, refer to a meaning limited to the area of Islamic Law in reference to the former, or that the meaning of the latter term is limited to a great struggle in the sense of a 'holy war'. This is not what is meant. Both meanings of the aforementioned terms are intimately connected. The great effort and struggle referred to, is directed towards the self, because:

"Although the human being is created in "the best of moulds", but without true faith and good works he is worse than the lowly beasts. It is against these non-beneficial aspects of the animal powers that the Holy Prophet urged us when he alluded to the greater struggle (*jihād*) of man, for they are the enemy within."[21]

Some may question us, asking how can we assert that the meaning of the term *jihād* employed by the Prime Minister in his speech, does not refer to the narrow interpretation to mean 'holy war'? We will answer, that according to the Prime Minister, "the concept of jihad must be given a broader interpretation, covering all aspects of life, including the pursuit of knowledge, the mastery of science and technology and economic activity".[22] From this, it is clear that the meaning of the term *jihād* is not limited. Again, similar to the explanation with reference to the term *karāmāt* alluded to in the chapter concerning Abdullah Fāhim, there are

---

[21] *Prolegomena*, 146.
[22] See the Prime Minister's keynote address delivered at the UMNO General Assembly on the 23rd of September 2004 in Kuala Lumpur.

several ranks (*marātib*) of *jihād*, the lowest of which is understood to mean 'holy war'. The more noble rank is characterised by the struggle in pursuit of true knowledge (*'ilm*).[23] Then there is the most noble rank, which represents the struggle against the bestial nature of man. It is this struggle which the Prime Minister refers to.

So now we return to our task at hand, and that is to explain what is meant by the Prime Minister when he speaks of 'Islam hadhari'. If one were to follow the arguments put forth in the preceding chapters, one may conclude that what the Prime Minister is advocating is a shift towards *understanding the present age in the framework of Islām*. If the phrase 'Islam hadhari' is understood as such, then there can be no confusion, both on the part of the Muslim opposition or on the part of the allied opposition. Accusations from the aforementioned, condemning UMNO of trying to propagate a new 'religion', will not arise. Therefore, if we were to construct a true definition of what is meant by the phrase 'Islam hadhari', it would read *fahm al-ḥāḍir fī īṭār al-Islām*, or **understanding the present age in the framework of Islām**. This is what we believe is *truly* meant by the Prime Minister. The only way to achieve this is to once again

---

[23] We must remain cautious in correctly defining what we mean. We have understood knowledge here to correspond with the Arabic *'ilm*, to distinguish between what is prevalent today in terms of employing vogue terminology without adequate or correct designation. What we mean, is that we do not agree that the term 'knowledge' be used in phrases like 'knowledge based economy', or 'knowledge based government' etc. because what is meant here is not *'ilm*. What is meant is *ma'lūmāt*, which corresponds to information or data in the English language.

emulate the intellectual tradition of Islamic thought, whose very foundations are premised on the ability to make sound, valid definitions. We are reminded that "Islām demands the mastery of science".[24] Therefore, it is important to remember that Islām, as defined by its worldview, does not merely refer to the ritualistic aspect.

---

[24] See the Prime Minister's keynote address delivered at the UMNO General Assembly on the 23rd of September 2004 in Kuala Lumpur.

Epilogue

THE PRECEDING CHAPTERS represent our attempt to comprehend and propose a plausible and meaningful response to the current dilemma centred around the phrase 'Islam hadhari'. We have done so, beginning with the Prime Minister's intentions as a template, after which we have constructed founded upon what we know concerning the Prime Minister, his heritage, and his expressed concern for both the Malays in particular and the Muslims in general, what we believe to be the most reasonable, adequate explanation of his ideas which would allow for the arrival of intelligible meaning in the soul. In addition, we have attempted to show, by way of adopting the inherent meanings couched in the Prime Minister's poetic composition, that the Muslims are suffering from a loss of identity exacerbated by an ignorance towards not only Islām, but an ignorance towards the worldview of Islām, history and an inability to make definitions.

ABDULLAH AHMAD BADAWI

Indeed, the questions posed to al-Ghazzālī were of the
nature of the One True Reality, His existence and essence,
the fate of the soul, heaven and hell, principles and foundations of the *sharī'ah*, the nature of man and so on. These
were the issues that gripped the Muslim world more than
one thousand years ago. Yet, how do some of these same
issues manage to confront man in modern times? Has not al-
Ghazzālī dispatched with the frivolities of ignorance? As is
perhaps an altogether frequent injustice, al-Ghazzālī suffered
the calumniation and condemnation of those opposed to him
simply by virtue of his vast intellect. But then, such is the
not unknown nature of man. Even today, the followers of
Ibn Taymiyyah continue to ignore his great contributions,
going so far as to belittle his augmentation of the stock of
knowledge and accuse him of being the source for Muslim
decline with regard to the sciences. We, on the other hand,
believe the contrary, that it was al-Ghazzālī who was wholly
responsible for the revivification of the tradition of learning
and inquiry. In addition, we believe that it is the followers of
Ibn Taymiyyah who should be held partially responsible for
the failure of Muslims with regard to the sciences. The
inability of Ibn Taymiyyah to fully appreciate and understand the arguments presented by al-Ghazzālī, in defence of
Islām, caused him to completely overlook the importance of
reason, which is perhaps one of the criteria responsible for
the inability of the mind of the modern Muslim to conceptualise adequate definitions.

Overwhelming interest in so called 'scholars' from the
Indian subcontinent and other parts of the modern Muslim
world has only perpetuated the condition we refer to as

'intellectual catatonia'. The seemingly fervent passion by the local universities and institutions of learning for employing the works of Mawdudi, Abu Hassan al-Nadwi and Hassan al-Banna throughout the preceding decades, for example, have not left the indelible imprint of intellectualism desired. Perhaps this is due to the fact that the aforementioned scholars are more commonly known for their political activism. The Prime Minister, in advocating a plausible response, seeks to once again revive the intellectual tradition synonymous with learning and advancement. Therefore, the age of activism and feeble mindedness must be consigned to the annals of history.

In our time therefore, answers to problematic questions must coincide with a profound grasp of the modern era in terms of its ideological milieu and history of its passage. Religion, aided by the confines of reason in tandem with a correct interpretation of the fundamental elements of the worldview, must be protected from the ravages of ignorance, otherwise the tendency to reduce everything to the law, akin to what the Jews have done with their religion, will continue unabated. What are these answers to the questions we speak of? Some of the more problematic questions for the government concern how we embrace globalisation, for instance. How do we embrace globalisation according to the framework of the worldview of Islām? Are some of its principal intentions antithetical to Islām and the worldview? Malaysia intends to be a centre for conflict resolution, yet according to the United Nations in their attempts to promote and export their ideals, "individuals must not only be free to criticise the religion into which they are born, but also to reject it for another or to remain without one".[1] How do we become the centre for conflict resolution if we are in conflict with the ideals and proposals forwarded by international bodies like the United Nations? More importantly, how does one reconcile this statement as it is clearly the antithesis to the tenets of the worldview of Islām? We may cite another example concerned with economics in general, and with money and banking in particular. The current definitions with regard to money and interest remain problematic. What is it that defines wealth? What is it that constitutes *riba*? In this regard, we have long accepted the opinions of those aforementioned activists from the Indian subcontinent, Mawdudi in particular. Now, after long last, we must ask this question. Is the current definition concerning *riba* adequate? Or are there other possibilities which would allow one to embrace the progressive platform espoused by the Prime Minister.[2] What we have mentioned thus far is just by way of example. Suffice it to say however, these are the kinds of questions requiring answers. They cannot be answered merely by institutionalising a set of misunderstood laws.

Failure to recognise the fact that in institutionalising laws that should already be inculcated when young, fractures the institution of authority. Today we are gradually becom-

---

[1] See United Nations, United Nations Development Programme, *Human Development Report 2004* (New York: United Nations, 2004).

[2] We are of the opinion that the current definition with regard to *riba* is grossly inadequate stemming from a narrow minded perception and intellectual incapacity. There exists other definitions, for instance, see Fazlur Rahman, "Riba and Interest", *Islamic Studies*, v. III, 1964.

ing aware of the problems facing us. Sadly, this realisation is not being adequately understood in the intended manner. The onus of accountability is largely ignored. The burden of responsibility is passed down as it were, to the young, thereby absolving one in a position of authority of any accountability. And the same misguided practice persists. Ideas whose meanings are not immediately apparent are relegated to the realm of mere slogan; as a result, subsequent generations soon forget, choosing instead to ascribe one idea or another to the domain of mere political platform. These ideas, if ignored, then take up residence in the archives where they remain until history repeats itself, but we have previously mentioned that the very proponents of certain ideas, are of the opinion that history and philosophy are no longer relevant.

By learning from history, by advocating a revival in the Islamic sciences and Islamic thought in general, in order to advance the understanding of Islām with reference to the Malays, *this* is what part of the struggle of UMNO should be. The Muslim intellectual tradition should be taken advantage of and not cast to the wayside strewn alongside ignorance, waste and despair. The establishment of an intellectual tradition will ultimately result in the establishment of authority and an intelligent society. This is true democracy in Islām. And so our task of understanding the present age cast in the framework of Islām will be complete, Inshā' Allāh.

Bibliography

Abdullah Ahmad Badawi. *Managing Success.* Petaling Jaya: Pelanduk Publications, 2003.

Açikgenç, Alparslan. *Scientific Thought and its Burdens.* Istanbul: Fatih University Publications, 2000.

Akdoğan, Cemil. "Muslim Influence upon European Scholarship and Learning". *Al-Shajarah, Journal of the International Institute of Islamic Thought and Civilization* (ISTAC), 6 no.2 (2001): 161-196.

Al-Attas, Syed Muhammad Naquib. *Islām and the Philosophy of Science.* Kuala Lumpur: International Institute of Islamic Thought and Civilization [ISTAC], 1989.

_____ *On Quiddity and Essence.* Kuala Lumpur: International Institute of Islamic Thought and Civilization (ISTAC), 1990.

_____ *The Intuition of Existence.* Kuala Lumpur: International Institute of Islamic Thought and Civilization (ISTAC), 1990.

_____ *Islām and Secularism.* Kuala Lumpur: International Institute of Islamic Thought and Civilization (ISTAC), 1993. (1st edition 1978).

_____ *The Degrees of Existence.* Kuala Lumpur: International Institute of Islamic Thought and Civilization (ISTAC), 1994.

_____ *Prolegomena to the Metaphysics of Islām. An Exposition of the Fundamental Elements of the Worldview of Islām.* Kuala Lumpur: International Institute of Islamic Thought and Civilization (ISTAC), 1995. (Reprint, 2001).

_____ *Islām dalam Sejarah dan Kebudayaan Melayu.* Kuala Lumpur: Angkatan Belia Islam Malaysia (ABIM), 1984. (1st edition 1972).

_____ *Islām: The Concept of Religion and the Foundation of Ethics and Morality.* Kuala Lumpur: Dewan Bahasa dan Pustaka, 1992. (1st edition 1976).

Ali, Abdullah Yusuf. *The Meaning of the Holy Qur'ān.* Brentwood, Maryland: Amana Corporation, 1994. (1st edition 1989).

Barnes, Jonathan (ed.). *The Complete Works of Aristotle.* Princeton: Princeton University Press, 1995.

Burckhardt, Titus. *Mirror of the Intellect.* Albany: State University of New York Press, 1987.

Burrell, David. "Aquinas and Islamic and Jewish Thinkers". *The Cambridge Companion to Aquinas.* Norman Kretzmann and Eleonore Stump (eds.). Cambridge: Cambridge University Press, 1993: 60-84.

Ceric, Mustafa. *Roots of Synthetic Theology in Islām: A Study of the Theology of Abū Manṣūr al-Māturīdī.* Kuala Lumpur: International Institute of Islamic Thought and Civilization [ISTAC], 1995.

Dhanani, Alnoor. *The Physical Theory of Kalām: Atoms, Space and Void in Basrian Muʿtazilī Cosmology.* Leiden: E. J. Brill, 1994.

_____ "Muslim Philosophy and The Sciences". *The Muslim Almanac.* New York: Gale Research Inc., 1996: 189-204.

Fakhry, Majid. *A History of Islamic Philosophy.* New York: Columbia University Press, 1983.

Al-Ghazzālī, Abū Ḥāmid Muḥammad b. Muḥammad. *Maqāṣid al-Falāsifah.* Sulayman Dunya (ed.). Cairo: Dār al-Maʿārif, 1961. (Reprint).

_____ *Al-Munqidh min al-Ḍalāl.* Jamīl Salībā (ed.) Beirut: Dār al-Andalus, n.d.

_____ *Ihyāʾ ʿUlūm al-Dīn.* 5 vols. Beirut and Damascus: Dār al-Khayr, 1990.

Goodman, Lenn Evan. *Avicenna.* London: Routledge, 1992.

_____ *An Introduction to Medieval Islamic Philosophy.* New Haven, Connecticut: Yale University Press, 1988.

Gutas, Dimitri. "Aspects of Literary Form and Genre in Arabic Logical Works". *Glosses and Commenatries on Aristotelian Logical Texts: The Syriac, Arabic and Medieval Latin Traditions.* Charles Burnett (ed.). London: The Warburg Institute, University of London, 1993: 29-76.

Ibn Manẓūr, Jamāl al-Dīn Muḥammad ibn Mukarram al-Anṣārī. *Lisān al-ʿArab.* 18 vols. Beirut: Dār Iḥyāʾ al-Turāth al-ʿArabī, 1996. (Reprint).

Ibn Sīnā, Abū ʿAlī al-Ḥusayn. "Aqsām al-ʿUlūm al-ʿAqliyyah", *Tisʿu Rasāʾil.* Cairo[?]: Matbaʿah Hindiyyah biʾl Musikī, 1326AH lunar/1908.

_____ *Al-Ishārāt wa'l-Tanbīhāt*. Sulaymān Dunyā (ed.) Cairo: Dār al-Ma'ārif, 1958.

_____ *'Uyūn al-Hikmah*. 'Abd al-Rahmān Badawī (ed.). Beirut: Dar al-'Ilm, 1980. (Reprint).

_____ *Kitāb al-Shifā'*. Qanawāti et al. (ed.). Cairo: n.p., 1983. (Revised edition).

Inati, Shams Constantine. *Ibn Sīnā Remarks and Admonitions, Part One: Logic*. Toronto: Pontifical Institute of Medieval Studies, 1984.

_____ *Ibn Sīnā and Mysticism, Remarks and Admonitions: Part Four*. London: Kegan Paul International, 1996.

Al-Jurjānī, Al-Sayyid al-Sharīf 'Alī ibn Muhammad. *Kitāb al-Ta'rīfāt*. Beirut: Maktabah Lubnān, 1990.

Al-Kindī, Abū Yūsuf Ya'qūb b. Ishāq. *Rasā'il al-Kindī al-Falsafiyyah*. Muhammad 'Abd al-Hādī Abū Ridah [sic] (ed.). Cairo: Dār al-Fikr al-'Arabī, 1950.

Kamali, Sabih Ahmad. *Al-Ghazali's Tahafut al-Falasifah*. Lahore: Pakistan Philosophical Congress, 1963.

Kogan, Barry. *Averroes and the Metaphysics of Causation*. Binghamton: State University of New York Press, 1985.

Kraemer, Joel L. *Humanism in the Renaissance of Islam*. Leiden: E. J. Brill, 1986.

Kuhn, Thomas S. *The Structure of Scientific Revolutions*. Chicago: The University of Chicago Press, 1970. 2nd ed. (1st edition 1962).

Lindberg, David. *The Beginnings of Western Science: The European Scientific Tradition in Philosophical, Religious, and Institutional Context, 600 B.C. to A.D. 1450*. Chicago: The University of Chicago Press, 1992.

Al-Maqdisi, Muhammad Muflih. *Al-Ādāb al-Shar'iyyah*. Beirut: Al-Risalah Publishing House, 1997.

McCarthy, Richard Joseph. *Freedom and Fulfillment*. Boston: Twayne Publishers, 1980.

Mohamed Abid. *Reflections of Pre-Independence Malaya*. Petaling Jaya: Pelanduk Publications, 2004. 2nd ed. (1st edition 2003).

_____ *Imbasan Peristiwa-Peristiwa Sebelum Kemerdekaan Malaya*. Petaling Jaya: Pelanduk Publications, 2004. 2nd ed. (1st edition 2003).

Mokhtar Petah. *Abdullah Badawi: Pejuang Kemanusiaan Sejagat.* Kuala Lumpur: Pustaka Antara Sdn. Bhd., 1997.

_____ *Sheikh Abdullah Fahim: Penentu Tarikh Kemerdekaan Negara 31 Ogos '57.* Kuala Lumpur: Pustaka Antara Sdn. Bhd., 1997.

National Book Coucil of Malaysia. *National Book Policy.* Kuala Lumpur: Dewan Bahasa dan Pustaka, 1992.

Netton, Ian Richard. *Al-Fārābī and His School.* London and New York: Routledge, 1992.

Ng Tieh Chuan (ed.). *Mahathir Mohamad: A Visionary & His Vision of Malaysia's K-Economy.* Petaling Jaya: Pelanduk Publications, 2002.

Al-Qazwīnī, Najm al-Dīn al-Kātibī. "Matn al-Shamsiyyah", *Shurūḥ al-Shamsīyyah: Majmū'at Ḥawāshī wa Ta'līqāt. Al-Juz' al-Thānī.* Cairo: Sharikat Shams al-Mashriq, n. d., 287-309.

Rahman, Fazlur. *The Philosophy of Mullā Ṣadrā.* Albany: State University of New York Press, 1975.

_____ *Islam and Modernity.* Chicago and London: The University of Chicago Press, 1984.

_____ *Avicenna's Psychology.* Westport, Connecticut: Hyperion Press Inc., 1981.

_____ "Riba and Interest", *Islamic Studies*, v. III, 1964.

Rescher, Nicholas. *Studies in Arabic Logic.* Pittsburgh: University of Pittsburgh Press, 1963.

_____ *The Development of Arabic Logic.* Pittsburgh: University of Pittsburgh Press, 1964.

Senu Abdul Rahman (ed.). *Mental Revolution.* Adibah Amin (trans.). Petaling Jaya: Pelanduk Publications, 2004. (English translation of *Revolusi Mental.* Kuala Lumpur: Utusan Publications, 1971)

Sharif, Mian Mohammad. *A History of Muslim Philosophy.* 2 vols. Delhi: Low Price Publications, 1995. (Reprint).

Sprenger, Alois. "First Appendix to the Dictionary of the Technical Terms Used in the Sciences of the Mussalmans, Containing the Logic of the Arabians in the Original Arabic, with an English Translation". Calcutta: F. Carberry, Bengal Military Orphan Press, 1854, Asiatic Society of Bengal, Biblioteca Indica no. 88, 1-36.

(English translation of Najm al-Dīn al-Kātibī al-Qazwīnī's *al-Risālah al-Shamsiyyah*).

Tan, Cecilia. *Tun Sardon Jubir: His Life and Times*. Petaling Jaya: Pelanduk Publications, 1986.

Al-Tirmidhī, Abū 'Īsā Muhammad. *Sunan. Kitāb al-'Ilm, al-Kutub al-Sittah wa Shurūhuhā*. Istanbul: Cagri, 1992. (Reprint).

Al-Tabarī, Muhammad ibn Jarīr. *Jāmi' al-Bayān fī Tafsīr al-Qur'ān*. Beirut: Dār al-Ma'rifah, 1980.

Al-Tahānawī, Al-Shaykh al-Mawlawi Muhammad A'lā ibn 'Alī al-Farūqī. *Kashshāf Istilāhāt al-Funūn*. (2 vols). Lahore: Suhail Academy, 1993.

United Nations, United Nations Development Programme. *Human Development Report*. New York: United Nations, 2004.

Walzer, Richard. *Greek into Arabic*. Cambridge, Massachusetts: Harvard University Press, 1962.

_____ *Al-Farabi on the Perfect State: Abū Nasr al-Fārābī's Mabādi' Ārā' Ahl al-Madīna al-Fadīla*. Oxford: Clarendon Press, 1985. A revised text with introduction, translation, and commentary.

Wan Mohd. Nor Wan Daud. *The Educational Philosophy and Practice of Syed Muhammad Naquib al-Attas: An Exposition of the Original Concept of Islamization*. Kuala Lumpur: International Institute of Islamic Thought and Civilization [ISTAC], 1998.

Articles

Abdullah Ahmad Badawi, "Forwards Towards Excellence", UMNO President's opening address at the 55th UMNO General Assembly.

"Muslim World Needs a Meeting of Minds", *New Straits Times* (NST), October 2004.

NSTP Research and Information Service, "Spiritual Leader and UMNO Pioneer", *Sunday Mail*, November 2003.

Rose Ismail, "Just Reward for Mr. Nice Guy", *New Straits Times* (NST), November 2003.

"RTM to Screen Series on Islam Hadhari", *New Straits Times* (NST), September 2004.

Saiful Azhar Abdullah, "A Natural Successor", *New Straits Times* (NST), November 2003.

The Star, November 2003.

"Ummah Perlu Kuasai Fardu Ain, Kifayah", *Berita Harian*, September 2004.

Unpublished Theses

Al-Attas, Syed Ali Tawfik. *The Mashshā'ī Philosophical System: A Study, Commentary on and Translation of the Hidāyah al-Ḥikmah of Athīr al-Dīn al-Abharī.* A PhD thesis submitted to the International Institute of Islamic Thought and Civilization (ISTAC), September 2002.

Caksu, Ali. *Causality in History: Ibn Khaldun's and Hegel's Transformation of Aristotelian Causes.* A PhD thesis submitted to the International Institute of Islamic Thought and Civilization [ISTAC], February 1999.

Other Suggested Readings

Al-Attas, Syed Muhammad Naquib. *Risalah untuk Kaum Muslimin.* Kuala Lumpur: International Institute of Islamic Thought and Civilization [ISTAC], 2001.

_____ *The Oldest Known Malay Manuscript: A Sixteenth Century Malay Translation of the 'Aqā'id of al-Nasafī.* Kuala Lumpur: University of Malaya, 1988.

_____ *A Commentary on the Ḥ}ujjat al-Ṣiddīq of Nūr al-Dīn al-Rānīrī.* Kuala Lumpur: Ministry of Culture Youth and Sports, 1986.

Al-Attas, Sharifah Shifa (ed.). *Islam and The Challenge of Modernity. Proceedings on the Inaugural Symposium on Islām and the Challenge of Modernity: Historical and Contemporary Contexts, Kuala Lumpur, 1st-5th August 1994.* Kuala Lumpur: International Institute of Islamic Thought and Civilization (ISTAC), 1996.

Hng Hung Yong. *5 Men & 5 Ideas: Building National Identity.* Petaling Jaya: Pelanduk Publications, 2004.

Mahathir Mohamad. *The Challenge.* Petaling Jaya: Pelanduk Publications, 1986.

_____ *The Malay Dilemma.* Singapore and Kuala Lumpur: Times Books International, 1999. (1st edition 1970).

_____ *A New Deal for Asia.* Petaling Jaya: Pelanduk Publications, 2000.

_____ *The Malaysian Currency Crisis.* Petaling Jaya: Pelanduk Publications, 2000.

_____ *Malays Forget Easily.* Petaling Jaya: Pelanduk Publications, 2001.

_____ *Reflections on Asia.* Petaling Jaya: Pelanduk Publications, 2002.

_____ *Globalisation and The New Realities.* Petaling Jaya: Pelanduk Publications, 2002.

_____ *Reflections on Asean.* Petaling Jaya: Pelanduk Publications, 2003.

_____ *Mahathir Mohamad: Achieving True Globalisation.* Petaling Jaya: Pelanduk Publications, 2004.

Mohamad Najib Abdul Razak. *Defending Malaysia: Facing the 21st Century.* London: Asean Academic Press, 2002.

Al-Roubaie, Amer. *Globalization and the Muslim World.* Petaling Jaya: Malita Jaya Sdn. Bhd., 2002.

Index